David

MASTERING
CHURCH
MANAGEMENT

MASTERING
CHURCH
MANAGEMENT

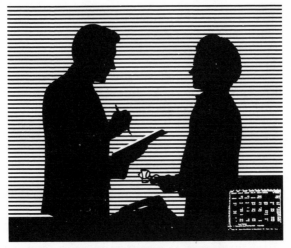

Don Cousins
Leith Anderson
Arthur DeKruyter

MULTNOMAH
Portland, Oregon 97266

Christianity Today, Inc.

MASTERING CHURCH MANAGEMENT
© 1990 by Christianity Today, Inc.
Published by Multnomah Press
Portland, Oregon 97266

Multnomah Press is a ministry of Multnomah School of the Bible, 8435 N.E. Glisan Street, Portland, Oregon 97220.

Printed in the United States of America.

Library of Congress Cataloging-in-Publication Data

Anderson, Leith.
        Mastering church management / Leith Anderson, Don Cousins,
    Arthur DeKruyter.
            p. cm.
        ISBN 0-88070-338-5
        1. Church management. I. Cousins, Don. II. DeKruyter, Arthur H.
    III. Title.
    BV652.A68   1990
    254—dc20   90-31857
                                                                     CIP

    91 92 93 94 95 96 97 98 99 - 10 9 8 7 6 5 4 3 2

CONTENTS

Introduction

If economics is called "the dismal science," management qualifies as "the disparaged science." Popular images of administrators as either balding bureaucrats counting paper clips or domineering dictators barking orders don't help the cause. Even visions of coolly efficient CEO's commanding their steel-and-glass corporate temples damage the concept for those interested in *ministry*.

Yet any minister with more than a month's experience understands the role management plays in pastoral effectiveness:

● Faced by more tasks than ever can be accomplished, pastors must learn to prioritize.

• Called upon to participate in congregational decisions of major consequence, pastors must gain discernment.

• Charged with equipping the saints to minister, pastors must develop expertise in training and delegation.

• Besieged by forces and personalities, sometimes at odds with one another, pastors must diplomatically structure ways for people to work together.

• Affected by societal and religious trends, pastors must learn to exegete culture to plan intelligently.

Let's face it: a pastor who cannot manage the ministry will find it filled with frustration and discouragement.

Mastering Church Management

When the editors of LEADERSHIP survey pastors in each edition of the journal, we often ask the question: What has been the toughest part of ministry for you? The answers are varied, but we always can count on some like these:

— Coming to terms with my ministry role.

— Time management: choosing and accomplishing the truly important tasks.

— Recruiting willing workers.

— Leading the church through change.

— Enlisting the best qualified laity for responsible positions.

—⁻ Motivating and equipping lay people to minister among the lost.

Certainly questions of faith and theology accompany these interests, but questions of leadership and management always shoulder their way to the fore. No pastor wants to just do the job; he or she wants to do it competently, responsibly, effectively. Hence the interest in church management.

That's why this second volume of the Mastering Ministry series looks at management. The first volume in the series covered preaching, and successive volumes will illumine evangelism, worship, pastoral care, and a number of other topics. But no matter how *informed* a church leader can become in any of these fields, *effectiveness* depends, to a large extent, on management.

Let's pause a moment to say that none of the techniques or ideas in this book is meant to replace the empowerment of the Holy Spirit. The best management with no Spirit equals nothing. The most gifted manager who lacks spiritual power may run a nice organization, but it won't be an effective church. All the same, however, if all truth is God's truth, then the Spirit can aid the church's ministry through sound management practices. Wise will be the practitioner who utilizes the best of God's management truth.

We can't claim divine inspiration for the chapters that follow, but we are enthusiastic about the insight and counsel offered. Our confidence comes from the caliber of our three authors, each of whom brings proven experience into this undertaking. Two have helped grow churches from scratch, and the third has helped revitalize a declining institution. Let me introduce you to them individually.

Leith Anderson

Leith Anderson is a pastor and a student of the art and science of church leadership. He pursued his education at Moody Bible Institute, Bradley University, and Denver Seminary, and he added to it with a Doctor of Ministry degree from Fuller Theological Seminary. Ten years at Calvary Baptist Church in Longmont, Colorado, gave Leith his early ministry experience, and today he teaches occasional courses on church management at Bethel Seminary in St. Paul, Minnesota.

Since 1977, Leith has served as senior pastor of Wooddale Church in Eden Prairie, a suburb of Minneapolis. His tenure there hasn't been quiet. Those years have witnessed a relocation to a new site, a change of the church's name, and the growth of the congregation to around double the number when Leith arrived. These massive changes could not have taken place as smoothly without the sensitive, informed management Leith provided.

To be sure, Leith is intent on informed practice. He wants to know why something does or doesn't work, so he does his homework. He's as knowledgeable about the maximum distance people can discern facial expressions (see Chapter 8) as he is about ministry skills. He can talk about acoustics or the Atonement, sanctuary aesthetics or early ascetics — with equal interest.

Talking with him, you get the feeling he greatly enjoys making the church effective in every aspect. After all, what other church do you know whose pastor has created a crisis-response team — complete with spokespersons for the media, and influential, discerning church leaders — to handle whatever eventualities may arise, such as a tornado or a church fire or a far-off missionary needing a medevac helicopter?

His church aligns itself to the statement: "The purpose of Wooddale Church is to honor God by bringing lives into harmony with him and one another through fellowship, discipleship, and evangelism, based upon the Bible as a standard." Most of the people at Wooddale Church could at least paraphrase the three distinctives.

But Leith wants that and more: "We're far more concerned that people *experience* fellowship, discipleship, and evangelism than that they can *articulate* it." This concern, in the final analysis, separates Leith from a mere theorist; he makes sure the practice of good management leads to a church of people experiencing the gospel and doing the work of Christ. Leith would be the first to concede there are loose edges in his — as in any — congregation, but he has a plan to bind them up. You can expect it.

Don Cousins

Don Cousins is a home-grown product of the earlier ministry from which Willow Creek Community Church sprouted. When Bill Hybels, Willow Creek's pastor, began leading the Son City youth ministry in Park Ridge, Illinois, one of his most promising protégés was a high school student named Don Cousins. In 1975, Don moved with Bill to the rented theater building in which Willow Creek Community Church was founded. Since then, he has been active in all aspects of the church's development into a nationally heralded congregation attracting 13,000 people weekly to services in its state-of-the-art facility in South Barrington, Illinois.

Don now serves as associate pastor, a position in which he directs 80 of the more than 225 staff members and oversees the ministry directors who keep about ninety subministries afloat at Willow Creek. He has founded several of the ministries and then worked himself out of the job by tapping and training the people who took over the positions. A voracious seeker of ideas, Don has augmented his formal education (a B.A. in biblical studies from Trinity College in Deerfield, Illinois) by reading widely the secular texts most affecting management. He's as at home quoting Peter Drucker as Peter the apostle. Don also has surrounded himself with capable counsel from the staff and elders. Thus, he has grown continually with a ministry responsibility that keeps mushrooming.

Don is a gracious man, but he remains single-minded about one thing: evangelism, or "reaching Nonchurched Harry" as it is referred to around Willow Creek. And that makes him sold on excellence. "Good management makes for excellence," he believes, "and I don't want to settle for anything less. Why? Because of evangelism.

"Unbelievers are attracted to what is done well, whether it's in church programming, the layout of the facilities, or the cleanliness of the building. And once they are drawn to excellence in the church, they can be drawn to the Author of excellence."

Don beats the drum for excellence because, as he says, "people rarely view churches as first-rate organizations. They demand greatness from sports franchises, the media, and the entertainment industry. But a church — well, it's just a church. People almost expect the slide projector to break down and the piano to fall out of tune. Because of this stereotype, I redouble my efforts to achieve excellence at Willow Creek."

His stamp is seen throughout Willow Creek. It's imprinted on the organizational structure and the well-planned facilities, but most of all it's reproduced in the hearts and lives of the people with whom Don works. One comes away from Willow Creek with a new understanding of the proverb: The man who says it cannot be done should not interrupt the man doing it.

Arthur DeKruyter

"A pastor who gets things done — well" is one way to describe Arthur DeKruyter. He's a sure-minded, proactive, in-charge kind of pastor, a ministerial entrepreneur in the best sense of the word.

This characteristic began at an early age as Arthur grew up in a family that operated a retail hardware store. There he picked up the, ahem, nuts and bolts of managing even the small details of an operation. "I learned you had to pay attention to little things, or problems would result," he recalls.

His education continued at Calvin College and then at Calvin Theological Seminary in Grand Rapids, Michigan. There he received his Th.B. degree. Later Princeton Theological Seminary granted him a Th.M., and Westminster College in New Wilmington, Pennsylvania, conferred a D.D. degree.

Right out of Princeton, Arthur accepted a call to Western Springs Christian Reformed Church in suburban Chicago, where he pastored over thirteen years. Then in 1965 the entrepreneurial spirit rose when he was called to found a new church in Oak Brook, an affluent suburb of Chicago. From just a handful of families meeting in a school grew Christ Church of Oak Brook. The church constructed its first building in 1970, and it was filled by the second week. That characteristic growth has continued, and today more than 4,500 members call Christ Church home.

Such growth didn't come from a laissez faire pastor. In fact, Arthur thrives on activity. "The private areas of life for most people become church related to me," he confesses. "I read, think, pray, eat, and sleep with the church on my mind. A leisurely walk through a shopping center produces ideas for the ministry. A motion picture, a novel, or even a poignant life experience does the same." And he's unrepentant: "That is the way it should be; this is the responsibility of a leader."

His dedication to ministry is exemplified in the story he tells of his interest in vocal music: "I have a deep love for music. When I was nineteen, I was a soloist in a rather large production of Handel's *Messiah*. Upon ordination, I gave up performing, though I still found myself leading the church choir. Later at Christ Church, I realized I had to channel my energy fully into my primary work as pastor/administrator. So I gave up choir directing."

But in talking to Arthur, you get the feeling he counts it all joy. There is nothing he would prefer to what he's now doing: pastoring a thriving congregation and keeping it running right. He helped bring the church to the point it now occupies, and he has learned valuable lessons in the process, just as he did in the hardware store of his youth. It's those lessons he's happy to provide for our benefit.

Three Viewpoints

It won't take long to realize our three writers approach management from different viewpoints. As general editor, I'm glad they do, because that means we gain the advantage of three pronounced perspectives: three denominations of origin, three decades of birth, three distinct personalities, three sets of gifts and experiences. We've worked to give you the best from each man.

We realize you'll chew on what you like and toss out the rest, anyway, so we've provided a varied and hearty fare, solid nourishment for church leaders hungry to minister more effectively.

Bon appétit!

— *James D. Berkley*
senior associate editor
LEADERSHIP Journal
Carol Stream, Illinois

PART ONE
The Big Picture

I want to manage the church to God's glory. Anything less contradicts the Creator, who after creation surveyed his work and said, "It is good." He didn't say, "Oh, it'll do."

— Don Cousins

CHAPTER ONE
Grooming the Organization

F ew pastors graduate from seminary hoping to become administrators. The term *administration*, itself, hardly sets feet dancing. In many people's minds, *administration* stands precipitously close to *bureaucracy*. It smacks of endless details, of rigidity, red tape, and routine.

Yet, administration — managing the affairs of a church — often spells the difference between pastoral effectiveness and ineffectiveness.

The ministry philosophy of Willow Creek Community Church,

where I'm associate pastor, has been adopted by a number of other churches. One pastor, who started a ministry like ours several years ago, recently returned to Willow Creek.

"We duplicated Willow Creek's philosophy and strategy pretty well," he told me, "and that led us to about four hundred members. But now we've hit a wall."

He came back to figure out what was missing. Finally he discovered it. "I underestimated the role of leadership," he confessed. "I see now that strong, effective management is as important as the teaching gifts and the format of the services."

I couldn't agree more. While *administration* may be an unpopular word, the task of leading and managing a church effectively remains at the heart of ministry.

Management and Leadership

Management is one way leadership manifests itself in the church; it's leadership being implemented in the day-to-day operation of a complex organization.

One of the great biblical leaders was Nehemiah. He exhibited three abilities that every leader needs to develop and demonstrate.

First, a leader needs the discernment — the street sense — to assess *accurately* the current condition of the organization, to say, "This is where we are now." When Nehemiah looked at his countrymen, he saw people on the verge of losing their identity. Because Jerusalem was unprotected and vulnerable to attack, its inhabitants sought security in small villages outside the city. Gradually they melted into these foreign cultures, losing their unique language, culture, and religion.

Nehemiah had the discernment to assess the situation corectly. He saw beyond the obvious — that the Jews were drifting geographically — to the more subtle fact that they were drifting spiritually.

Second, a leader needs the vision and understanding to add, "And this is where we need to go." Nehemiah realized that Jerusalem needed a wall if it hoped to be the truly Jewish city God intended. Without a wall, the situation inevitably would worsen; the nation would lose whatever grip on godliness it had.

Visionary leaders know the status quo won't last forever; most static organizations are actually in the first stages of decline. So leaders look ahead. They envision change. Nehemiah pictured his nation as it ought to be — strong and sure of its identity. In his mind he "saw" the protecting wall.

Third, a good leader knows how to bring together the people and resources needed to move the organization from where it is to where it needs to be. Nehemiah was a master at this. He gathered together hundreds of workers and inspired them to work "with all their heart" (Neh. 4:6). When the completion of the wall was threatened by those who feared Israel's rise, Nehemiah organized half his laborers for battle. They would not give up their goal, even in the face of opposition.

Lead is an active verb. A leader is able to say, "Here's how we get to where we want to go," and people follow. Leadership is measured in great part by its ability to generate and direct movement.

As most good leaders know, management is the process of getting things done through other people. Even Boy Scout patrol leaders realize that leading doesn't mean personally doing all the fire building and pot cleaning. Good managers have the ability to bring together the necessary people and resources to accomplish the group's goals. They delegate responsibilities to those who can do the tasks with joy and excellence, so the jobs get done better than they themselves could have done them.

The Drawbacks of Being a Manager

Most workers fantasize about the bliss of being a manager. Authority, access to information, freedom to delegate work, and other perks make the position look inviting. But management is anything but easy. Consider the drawbacks:

— *Time.* Management obviously devours large chunks of time. It takes time to tune in to details; time to find, delegate, and train other workers; time to redirect a ministry or troubleshoot a problem.

We'd rather set up programs that run forever on their own. But that's like buying a car, driving it, and never doing anything to maintain it. Ministries, like cars, need regular maintenance and sometimes even replacement. People wear down. Leaders move away. Facilities become cramped or outdated. Methods lose their sparkle. Curricula don't work out.

Who has to deal with these, and scores of other problems? The manager. And that gobbles up time and energy.

— *Obscurity.* Many tasks a manager accomplishes get little notice. Preach a good message, and what happens afterward? People pat you on the back. Visit a grieving widow, and you earn the affection of her family and friends.

But what happens when the Christian education director, after much study, subtly changes materials to guarantee the quality of the Sunday school program? Or what is the response if you arrange to have the sidewalks swept and the main hallways vacuumed late Saturday nights to prepare for Sundays? Probably nothing. Managerial activities like those rarely draw accolades.

The summer before we added a second midweek service, I received a letter from a church member. He wrote, "Going to two weekday services in the fall may have a crushing effect on Bill [Hybels, the pastor]. Why don't you take more of the services?"

On the one hand, that was a compliment; he apparently appreciated my teaching gifts. On the other hand, he was saying, "Bill has too much to do; you certainly have time to ease his load." He had little appreciation for the management responsibilities that fill my days. He couldn't see my work directly, so he assumed I had little to do.

A person insecure about laboring in obscurity will find management an unsatisfying, thankless task. For me, the key to being a satisfied manager is to develop a spiritual perspective, to remind myself constantly that my heavenly Father, who sees in secret, knows what I'm doing. As I learn to be a God pleaser, and not a man pleaser, I find great joy in accomplishing the behind-the-scenes tasks that enhance the overall ministry of our church.

— *Tedium.* Management involves attending to details, and

because detail work is tedious, a manager needs to keep in mind the bigger picture. He needs to look down the road and say, "This may take longer now, but it will pay off in the long run."

Keeping budgets in line involves the tedium of poring over stat sheets, income projections, and expenditure requests. But careful evaluations allow us to make sound decisions and give our church financial credibility. Likewise, I can't say I enjoy reviewing job descriptions, but it's a key to staff effectiveness and heads off time-consuming misunderstandings. So I'll bear the tedium now, because I know these tasks actually will prevent more work later.

— *Competing demands.* My job includes coming up with creative ideas, setting visionary goals, and initiating action. But too often I get pulled from the role of initiator to the role of responder — carrying out this request, solving this problem, greasing this squeaky wheel. When this happens, I get bogged down in the mire of competing demands and lose my ability to generate positive action.

My calendar is the clearest indicator of who's in control. Am I spending the majority of my day taking steps to reach predetermined goals? Or are ancillary tasks devouring the bulk of my time?

The key, of course, is to be perfectly clear about my goals. Any time I lose sight of them, or the steps necessary to reach them, I become vulnerable to competing demands. I'm on a string, moving at the whim of whomever pulls the hardest.

Another help is to establish "A priorities" and "B priorities." *A priorities* are the creative tasks I need to do to fulfill my ministry. They're proactive. They move the program, department, or ministry forward. *B priorities* are the tasks that merely support or supplement my main priorities. They're important, but they don't have the highest claim on my time.

For instance, I recently worked on a video of a training session for our leaders. To make that tape, someone had to attend to administrative details such as hiring a production crew, finding props, and arranging for refreshments breaks. Each of those things needed to be done — but not by me. Had I arranged every aspect of the taping, I would have had little time for preparing the message to be taped. My A priority was the message; the B priorities had to be delegated.

Another aspect of ministry I need to manage lest it overwhelm me is people issues: personal crises in leaders' lives, conflict between team members, or people who have outgrown their responsibilities and want a change. Scores of these management problems arise that demand consideration.

Most of us would like to ignore these situations and hope they heal themselves. They don't. We need to consider people problems an A priority and work proactively whenever possible. If we don't give these problems our attention, they'll end up demanding it in destructive ways. But if we handle the situations while they're small, they won't grow to the point where people get hurt. Nor will they capture us by surprise and devour unnecessary time and energy.

— *Detachment*. You enter the ministry because you love people, and then you spend your day reviewing budgets, evaluating programs, and purchasing curricula. Although a good manager quickly learns to delegate many of these tasks, there always will be managerial responsibilities that take us away from contacts with people. If we fail to appreciate the importance of troubleshooting a ministry, we will become frustrated by the detachment of managerial tasks.

On the other hand, good management rarely occurs in an interpersonal vacuum. So a good manager brings other people into the process. If I become unnecessarily detached as a manager — pushing papers and operating in an isolated realm of executive decision making — I deprive myself of the stimulation and giftedness of others, and deprive them of the satisfaction of contributing.

When I involve others in the managerial process, we solve problems jointly. We're "in the foxhole" together, and it gives us a sense of camaraderie. Meaningful relationships develop in the midst of doing ministry.

— *Exploitation*. Managers, responsible for incorporating others into the church's ministry, sometimes wonder if they're exploiting others. A few months ago, we hired a staff member from an environment in which he had operated pretty much as a Lone Ranger. He taught all the lessons, led the classes, and came up with the curriculum. I've been trying to help him realize that his present environment is bigger than he is. He can't do the whole job; he needs to solicit help from others.

When we discussed that, he mused, "Don't you sometimes feel you're using people?"

"Not in the ministry," I replied. "Giving people an opportunity to discover, develop, and use their gifts in ministry is doing them a favor. They gain the fulfillment of being God's instruments."

If I have to ask my friends to help me with a personal need — such as a home-maintenance project — I feel very uncomfortable. I find that kind of recruitment terribly difficult and always postpone it until the last minute. But when I'm asking people to serve the Lord, I don't hesitate or apologize. In fact, I believe it's one of the greatest gifts I can offer them.

The Value of Management

Being a manager has its drawbacks, but it's a challenge that gets my creative juices flowing day after day. Why? Because of these important contributions a manager makes:

— *Purpose and direction.* A manager is in a position to reaffirm purpose and direction for a ministry. If a ministry is not moving forward, it's probably moving backwards. Eventually it will become a victim of entropy, the tendency of anything to wind down, become random, move toward disorder. Managers can head off entropy by redefining purpose.

Years ago we set up a children's program, Promiseland, that adequately met our church needs. Over the years, however, it lost its effectiveness. Why? We hadn't managed it properly, and entropy had set in.

Our first step was to focus our purpose. Because Willow Creek draws many unbelievers who are not committed to weekly church attendance, we have many sporadic Promiseland attenders. So one of our primary goals in Promiseland was to provide a children's environment that was so inviting and enjoyable that the children would be excited about returning. We also wanted parents to have confidence in the care their children were receiving.

Reaffirming that goal helped us see how we had failed to reach it. We acknowledged that we were understaffed, our facilities were too cold and sterile to excite children, our curriculum didn't communicate effectively to the nonchurched, and our workers sensed a general lack of direction.

So we reassigned staff, made our general-purpose classrooms child centered on weekends, changed our curriculum, and made sure each of our teachers understood our goals. The results speak for themselves. Today children enjoy Promiseland more, parents see it as a tremendous benefit for their children, and both are attending more consistently. Through good leadership, we returned purpose to a faltering program.

— *Midcourse corrections*. Sometimes ministries need more than an affirmation of purpose; they need a whole new direction. They need leadership to take the wheel and turn the ship before it ends up in unwanted ports.

Some time ago our ministry to young singles, PrimeTime, reached the point where it couldn't grow because we had no appropriate facility big enough to accommodate a larger group. Even if we could have gathered more people under one roof, the large meetings would have been impersonal, and it would have been almost impossible to assimilate visitors or identify and train leaders.

It was time for a midcourse correction to better meet the needs of singles. We had to divide the ministry, forge manageable groups, locate and train new leaders, and shift facilities. Growth is a wonderful kind of problem, but it does force readjustments. In fact, this was the *fourth* time we had to steer a new course for PrimeTime. We're learning that most rapidly growing ministries need to be restructured once a year.

— *Increased effectiveness*. Simply put, good management enables a church to meet needs it couldn't meet otherwise.

Our ministry to older singles, Focus, provides a good example. Careful midcourse corrections have enabled Focus to grow steadily. As usual, with growth came increased financial support, more servants, and a broader pool of potential leaders. This opened the door for new ministries to start.

So Focus decided to start a branch of ministry specifically for single parents. As this ministry grew, it spawned a special ministry for children of single parents. And on it goes. Careful management leads to growth, to increased resources, to new ministries, and ultimately to more people's needs being met.

One nonchurched woman, a single parent, was struggling financially and had her hands full with two adolescent boys. A friend told her, "Go to Willow Creek; they'll help you." So she did. She attached herself to the single-parents' group, and her boys joined the children's group. Then our food pantry gave her food, our benevolence board helped her financially, and church members gave her rides to church when her car broke down. Over the months she's been overwhelmed by the love she's found and seems well on her way to becoming a Christian.

How could we have met that woman's needs if we hadn't been organized? We couldn't have. And if we had tried, it would have taken so much time, energy, and money, we would have vowed never to get involved again. But because the programs had developed as a natural result of management and growth, we were able to help her.

— *Increased scope.* Good management increases the number of people a church can reach. Personally, I could disciple eight to ten people a day — and then only if I scheduled them like an assembly line and didn't mind going home exhausted. Would it be possible to run my ministry that way? Yes. Would it be wise? Of course not. I'd be drained, and only a few people would be reached.

Carefully managing my ministry, however, helps me broaden the scope immensely. On an average day, I meet with three or four of our key staff and help them evaluate and organize their ministries. They in turn do the same for several other leaders who work with scores and scores of people every week. The breadth and depth of an organization's work depends on how it's managed.

McDonald's is a prime example. The original founders, the McDonald brothers, figured out how to produce a good product —

burgers and fries — and deliver them quickly. That was their genius. It worked so well in one store, they decided to franchise in their area. But they failed miserably. Why? They were great in the hands-on business of running their little store and cranking out a fast hamburger, but not so good at reproducing their method.

Enter Ray Kroc. He knew little about fast food, but he was an expert at franchising. He reproduced the McDonald brothers' operation at location after location. Ray's management of the organization enlarged its scope tremendously.

Similarly, the pastor who manages poorly may keep a small operation afloat through warmth and sincerity. But no matter how much he loves people or how fervently he preaches, the scope of his church will forever be limited to the few people he can associate with personally. The well-managed church, however, can provide the warmth and care of the small church in a multiplicity of organized subministries.

Signs of a Well-managed Church

1. A clearly defined purpose. There ought to be no mystery, no guesswork, about why a particular church body exists. Is it to be a loving Christian presence in a dark corner of the city? Then state it. Is it to present the claims of Christ to Nonchurched Harrys? Then let it be known in everything the church does. Is it to provide a place for worshiping the Living God in grandeur and power? Then go for it.

Whatever it is, the specific purpose of the church ought to be spelled out. The life of a church will be only as directed as its purpose, only as orderly as its philosophy and strategy.

2. A widely understood purpose. In a well-managed church, both the staff and congregation can articulate its purpose. Often the purpose statement has been reduced to a single sentence or a brief and memorable list. Willow Creek has a fourfold purpose: exaltation, edification, evangelism, and social action. This purpose is spelled out clearly in our membership classes, and once a year it is reiterated in a message at our midweek believers' service.

It's one thing for pastors to know clearly what the church's business is; it's another to impart that vision to those they lead so the people also own the vision. That's what Lee Iacocca did at Chrysler. He was a master at conferring the vision of a resurrected Chrysler to every employee. When they all understood the purpose and believed in it, they could work together enthusiastically to bring it about. When the purpose permeates every level of an organization, you know management is doing something right.

3. Servants who understand their unique contribution. In a well-run church, the individual players — the pastor, staff, elders and deacons, small-group leaders, and members — know their role in making the church's purpose a reality.

It's like a football team. The obvious purpose is to get the ball across the goal line. But unless the split end knows his route, and the left tackle his blocking assignment, and the center the snap count, they'll trip over each other and go nowhere. They need to know their specific assignments.

So it is in the church. If the worship leader doesn't know how much time he's allotted in the service, or if the youth minister doesn't know what activities he's expected to plan, or if the ushers aren't informed of special events, there will be disarray. In the well-managed church, these players not only know the overall purpose, they also know exactly what they can do to contribute to the goal.

4. A strategy that works. This may seem obvious, but it's equally obvious that some churches employ strategies that don't work. Let's say an American church wants to reach lost people. They adopt the strategy of singing on street corners, which has worked remarkably well in Brazil. But their efforts fail to win people in Minneapolis. Wise management will throw out that strategy and look for one that will work.

In fact, good management proposes, tries, refines, rethinks, scraps and starts over — whatever it takes to hit upon a strategy that bears fruit. Unless there is objective proof that the purpose is being fulfilled, the effective manager remains dissatisfied with any strategy. He keeps searching and experimenting until the ends of the church are met in a God-pleasing way.

5. Financial integrity. Since money is a major player in most church activities, the way it is raised, recorded, expended, and accounted for says much about the management of the church. When I see a ministry hurting financially because of irresponsible debt or ill-advised expenditures, I question the quality of management overall. But when a church runs a tight financial ship, even amid healthy challenges, I know it's well managed.

How money is handled also makes a statement to the unbelieving community. The church that invites people to inspect its audit and gives an accurate accounting of its expenditures will quiet the suspicions and inspire the confidence of the unchurched.

6. *A well-cared-for "Main Street."* Another sign of good management is a neat, clean, and attractive facility, especially those areas people pass through on Sunday morning — Main Street.

At Willow Creek, Main Street is the corridor from our entrance sign on the road, through our parking area, entrances, lobbies, and main halls, to our auditorium. It's the portion of our facilities everybody — and especially visitors — will traverse on Sunday. They may not see the offices or rehearsal rooms, just as guests in your home may not see your bedroom closet or the upstairs shower stall. But people at church will walk through Main Street.

Therefore, we give Main Street the same attention a host gives the front steps, living room, dining room, and bathroom prior to entertaining. Of course, we try to keep all our facilities neat and attractive, but in a pinch, Main Street gets the attention and resources. We want it to look inviting and pleasant.

Neglect of Main Street speaks volumes about a church's leadership. Managers who are careful about details such as these likely will have other aspects of the ministry under control.

The Case for Management

Not every pastor is gifted in church leadership. Some feel their call is to the Word and prayer, not to wrestling a congregation into organizational orderliness. Such pastors have two options: either find someone else to manage the church or learn to do it themselves. The third option of going without is unacceptable; the church lacking management will pay too great a price in ineffective evangelism, discouraged workers, and missed opportunities. So whether by inclination, delegation, or gumption, the work of leading a church must be accomplished.

But some think management is overrated these days. "We need more *pastors*," they say, "not an organization chart full of administrators!" So why should a *pastor* be concerned with management?

Theologically I can think of two reasons. First, we serve a God who deserves our best. He's given us the gifts and abilities to do ministry well, not just to muddle through. I want to manage the church to God's glory. Anything less contradicts the Creator, who after creation surveyed his work and said, "It is good." He didn't say, "Oh, it'll do."

Second, pastoral management best serves God's people. People are drawn to the brightest light. It would be wonderful to be a mega-watt searchlight, sweeping vast stretches of humanity, but few are called to that. Nonetheless, why be dull, 40-watt bulbs when we have the potential to be 200-watt beacons?

Management helps us make the most of the light we have. Organization helps us enhance our capabilities. If we order our lives well, and carefully manage those placed in our charge, our churches will shine brilliantly, as lights set on a hill.

*In a church, the stewardship of power is more important
than the stewardship of money.*

— Arthur DeKruyter

CHAPTER TWO
Stewardship
of Power

After a year and a half in my present ministry, I suddenly was
plunged into a crisis: four board members were leading a movement
to oust me. These were the turbulent days of the McCarthy era, and
the four trustees were convinced we should identify with a political-
ly ultra-conservative group. I insisted that the church was not a
political organization.

They questioned my priorities. They told me I was "unfit to
pastor the congregation."

"If you ask for my resignation and can explain your reasons to the congregation, I will do so," I replied. But they weren't willing to present their reasons publicly. So they appointed an investigating committee which eventually, of course, would find reason to get rid of me.

So I, along with two trustees who understood the situation, went to every family in the congregation that week. We told each one what was going on. Those four board members felt the pressure and left the church, eventually taking a quarter of the congregation with them.

That "solved" one problem but created another. With the departure of these four, our board was left without a quorum. We couldn't even hold a congregational meeting to elect a new board because only the board had the authority to call a congregational meeting.

Naturally, in such a divisive situation, I was concerned about who, in fact, legally controlled the assets of the church — the four dissident board members, who constituted a quorum, or the minority who remained. So I contacted an attorney and reviewed our church's constitution. I discovered that our constitution specified that the chairman of the board (in this case, the pastor) had full authority to act for the board in such an emergency.

That bit of information saved our fledgling congregation from a raw political power play. It was then that I first realized how important a constitution could be to a church.

As pastors, our first concern is to preach and pray, but we dare not remove ourselves from paying heed to the structure of a church. Good structure — like a constitution provides — is a fundamental element of the stewardship of power. And in a church, the stewardship of power is more important than the stewardship of money.

A church is both an organism and an organization. As it grows, the importance of proper structure grows with it. This demands careful attention to make sure power is properly channeled. That's one of the key functions of church management.

When I think of the proper stewardship of power, I think of the five laymen who, after that crisis, helped shepherd our church.

They were powerful individuals who could have led a battle against the preacher and probably won.

I was younger and needed training in administration. They were willing to help, and more important, they wanted me to succeed. They taught me how to use and distribute power. Let me share, then, some of the things they taught me, and some things I have learned elsewhere, about the stewardship of power.

Power Is a Trust

First, these wise individuals taught me that I was not entitled to power. The church did not belong to me, just as it did not belong to them. I learned to separate myself from the institution, as difficult as that was. They pointed out that power is fiduciary — entrusted to us by God and granted to us by the people we lead.

The call to ministry, and thus to a position of power, is part of a larger trust. To be ordained is to be accepted and authorized by the people of Jesus Christ. They delegate to the pastor the leadership of the body of Christ. We don't seize leadership or lay hands on ourselves. Rather, in ordination, a group of Christians in effect say, "We believe this person is qualified and possesses a sense of divine calling. We acknowledge that calling and have, therefore, asked him to perform a specific task among us."

Thus, along with our authority to proclaim the Word of God to the people, we also have the obligation to manage the authority and power handed us. It is a power derived from God, yes, but through his people. In short, power is a trust, to be used, not for myself, but on behalf of the church.

Power Is Accountable

Those five leaders also impressed upon me the responsibility power brings with it to be always accountable, either to a person or to a group. I cannot function independently of God's people. Not even strong congregational loyalties to the pastor should short-circuit personal accountability.

A particular danger threatens pastors, such as me, who have

founded a church: the temptation to abuse the power naturally accumulated. After all, nearly everyone likes my way of doing things or they would not have joined this church and remained members. But therein lies the potential for abuse. People will not readily challenge me publicly or privately if they have respected my leadership for years.

Therefore, in my case, I am careful to be accountable to my board. This groups understands the vision of Christ Church, but they are strong, independent thinkers. They can ask me any question — and do! They can disagree with me and vote against my wishes. And I am willing to take their discipline when they feel it necessary. I encourage such independence of thought and action; it keeps me accountable.

Our building committee was formulating plans for a new kitchen some time ago. They had consulted professionals, but I felt their plan had serious flaws. We'd had a lot of problems in the previous kitchen, and I didn't want them repeated. Time and again, I strongly stated my case to them, to no avail; the building committee chairman and the architect had other ideas. I could have continued to campaign against the plans, but I recognized the authority of the board. If the board had considered all the evidence, and if the board was persuaded to go with the architect's plan, I wasn't going to keep arguing.

Accountability also means I must be open with the board; I must never be covert or keep secrets.

For example, sometimes ministers are given exceptional gifts from members of the congregation. The temptation for pastors is not to let anyone know. Once a member offered to give a used car to one of our staff pastors. The pastor told the member he'd have to consult the board. The board safeguards our staff because we make sure they know about such gifts. Why? When people have given special gifts, it's easy to afford those people special treatment. But we want to be fair to both poor and rich, to those who have given gifts and those who haven't. We long to obey the command of James not to honor above others the fellow with the golden ring. By letting others in on the decision whether to accept these kinds of gifts, we minimize that danger.

This principle applies whether I'm deciding who I perform a wedding for, or who uses the building, or whether someone can borrow the church's video equipment for personal use. The rules of the organization must be observed without exception. The minute I start making exceptions and giving preferential treatment to some, I sacrifice integrity. That's a definite misuse of power.

If someone seeks preferential treatment, then firm consistency becomes the best policy. If I am consistent, people will learn to expect it and trust me.

Of course, when I turn down inappropriate requests, the people sometimes fume because I refused to bend the rules for them. But in the long run, it's still a better policy. Eventually they accept it and perhaps even respect me, assured that no one else will likely manipulate me. That is important in a church, for seeking favoritism is nothing more than a power play in disguise.

Power Is to Be Delegated

When I delegate responsibility, at the same time I must delegate the power to perform it. Furthermore, I never withdraw that power without clearly saying so.

If a father, dissatisfied with the preschool class, approaches me, insisting that I change preschool teachers, for instance, I remind him that I don't run that department. I then refer him to the proper person.

If he says, "I've already talked to the Christian education chairwoman, and she doesn't want to listen," I reply, "Well, she runs the department, not me. I'll discuss the matter with her, but if she doesn't want to change teachers, I guess they won't be changed."

I expect that same respect to prevail among staff members. To function as a team, we have to respect the power for which each of us has jurisdiction. When we design job descriptions for staff members and volunteer workers, we must give them the power to do the job. We cannot keep a tight rein and at the same time expect staff members to succeed.

Practicing the Stewardship of Power

Several steps are helpful in practicing the proper stewardship of power.

1. Discover the church's center of power. Woe to us if we don't know where power lies in a church. That may not always be evident. But rest assured, someone or some group possesses the power that runs that institution. Who actually holds the reins? What are their objectives? Are those in power willing to share it with others, or do they keep it for themselves? Only after locating the epicenter of authority can we help decide how power will be distributed in the church.

Our church holds a workshop on church administration each year. For several years, we inadvertently encouraged young pastors to attempt things they could not accomplish. The pattern went something like this: The young leaders return from the church administration workshop charged up with new ideas and fresh dreams. But when the harsh reality of the church's vested interests, traditions, and power structure greets them at the door, their plans fizzle and their vision dies. Nothing they had envisioned will happen because certain members or committees are not willing to share power. The pastors, naturally frustrated, plunge into the center of the controversy, and their stress level mushrooms. The result, all too often, is clergy burnout.

Such a bleak scenario need not occur. Wisely and patiently discovering the epicenter of power will help open closed doors.

I came out of a denomination in which power was shared differently than it is in my present church. It was a polity established by a denomination. Many still are not ready to give up their old system of sharing power. As a result their growth is stymied.

People frequently call asking for the name of a dynamic young minister to serve their congregation. In many cases, I know that if a minister goes to their church, he will be handcuffed. Even the best managers will fail if their church will not share power.

After taking the time to locate the center of church power, the next step is to begin working with it.

2. Discuss the unmentionable. It is not easy to talk about power with a strong board or dominant members. Yet, it is best to raise the issue head-on. Though it may be threatening, we should begin with one-on-one discussions with individuals who wield power in the church.

I say "individuals" because power rarely resides in a group — not even in the official church board. Power usually resides in individuals.

The man who has funded a number of projects may be the dominant influence, for instance. Money can buy such power. If such a person dislikes an idea, the issue dies. It makes little difference how much time or effort a committee puts into a proposal if the "church boss" chooses to shoot it down. One powerful person can easily dominate a group.

To redeem the situation, I initiate discussions with the person or persons possessing power. Do they know their own influence? I attempt to discover what motivates these individuals. What do they intend to do with their power? What are their objectives?

Next I try to disciple these individuals on the proper use of power, helping them understand from a biblical perspective what their responsibility is with their power. If a pastor can help such individuals see the importance of the stewardship of power, the whole church is strengthened.

With one "church boss," for example, I began by finding a way to have breakfast with him. I impressed upon him the amount of leadership he was exerting in the church, which, I continued, carried with it a great deal of power. He readily acknowledged that. I explained that this is a great trust from God, and that power could be used to bless or harm a congregation. By establishing a relationship in an informal setting and discussing forthrightly the issue of power, I helped this man recognize his role, and we learned to work together.

3. *Ask for help in managing power.* Not all pastors are equally gifted in managing power. Some find it easy; others struggle. Christian organizations begun by visionaries often have encountered trouble as they grew. The problem was not incapable leaders, but leaders who did not know they were incapable in administration.

Visionary leaders often need help from others gifted in management and administration. Even pastors with little talent for administration can survive and prosper if they let others help them develop expertise.

Or perhaps they can delegate administrative tasks to someone else. A staff member or lay volunteer can handle areas of administration on their behalf.

Peter Drucker, the management expert, once said that the minute you hire your first secretary, you have an organization. Learning to manage takes time and may require ministers to seek guidance. But it is time well spent. The survival of a church or personal ministry may depend upon it. Time invested now could mean a crisis avoided tomorrow.

4. Use power in a pastoral way. There are times when a minister's power is to be used directly and forcefully, to uphold church doctrine or to be faithful to church policy. That's why it's entrusted to us. But even during such crises, power can be wielded with a pastoral touch.

In my first church, a small congregation of thirty-five families, there was one successful businessman who provided a large percentage of the church's income. When things needed doing — painting, plumbing, repairs — the congregation would raise some of the money, and he would pay the rest. Everyone knew about this because he made sure they knew about it. Naturally, it gave him an enormous amount of power.

When I arrived at the church, I discovered six days before our quarterly Communion service that, although the congregation was served Communion in individual cups, this man and his family were served from a common cup. An elder would serve them separately from the rest of the congregation.

When I heard about this, I reacted strongly, "Wait a minute. This, of all times, is a time of unity. Why are we divided in our taking of Communion?" Because I was caught unawares, I went along with it that first Sunday.

Before the next Communion service, however, I went to the elders and explained why this procedure wasn't good for this church. I discovered that the congregation had voted some time before to use individual cups, but the board had never enforced the policy with this family.

I then told them, point blank, "I am not going to serve this family Communion this way again. Furthermore, I think that you elders need to tell this family that it isn't going to happen here again. I'd like someone to make a motion to support what the congregation has decided." So they voted to affirm the congregation's action. Then I said, "Now, who is going to go and tell these people?" Naturally, nobody wanted to go.

"Well," I continued, "I will go if one of you will go with me. And I'll do the speaking." One of them agreed.

So we went. Here I was, a 25-year-old pastor, sitting across from a man of 60 in the middle of his magnificent and richly appointed house. The whole family was there: the man, his wife, a bachelor son, and a single daughter.

I told them that I understood the congregation had voted to take Communion from individual cups and that I thought it was important to be united in our practice. Therefore, we weren't going to be using the common cup anymore in our church. As expected, I received a serious dressing down: "Who do you think you are to come and disturb things? This has been done for years. The common cup is more meaningful to us. You are wrong to take away this expression of our faith."

I said, "Well, the board of elders unanimously voted to uphold the decision of the congregation, which was nearly unanimous to begin with, except for your family. Now we intend to put this policy into practice."

"Then, we'll have to leave the church," the father said. I tried to keep my voice calm and matter-of-fact as I said, "And where would you like us to send your membership?"

Everything got quiet. No one had ever spoken to them like that before. This family did not believe the church could exist without them. When they realized, however, that I meant what I said, to the point of seeing them go, they said, "Let us pray about it. We'll think about it." So, that's the way we left it.

All week I wondered what they would do, but they came back to church the next Sunday, and the Sundays following. The week before the next Communion, however, the man and his son showed up at the elders' meeting. They came to protest, to ask if we would serve them in a common cup the next Sunday. We said we felt we needed to honor the decision of the congregation and to be unified in our practice. We would not serve them separately.

Then the man said, "Your decision presents a serious spiritual problem for my family. The biblical practice is to drink from a common cup. If we use individual cups, we will be held accountable by our Lord at the Day of Judgment."

I wasn't going to reverse the church's decision, but in light of their concern, I suggested a way out. We would record on the books of the church that the church was responsible for this family using individual cups, that if there was any wrong in this practice, the church would be at fault, not them. And we as a board were willing to assume responsibility before the Lord for that. So we included in the minutes of that board meeting that this family was exonerated from any guilt in the matter.

Most of the congregation was aware of the dispute, of course, so the next Sunday, everything was tense. But we served everyone individual cups. The family took Communion with everyone else that Sunday and every time after that. The issue was settled.

Power, then, is a trust. At times it must be used forthrightly to carry out the will of Christ and his church. But good stewardship of power requires that we use it with tact and care.

*Administration does not keep me from people. It is
people. It doesn't prevent my serving them; it gives me a
way to serve them.*

— Leith Anderson

CHAPTER THREE
Staying People Centered and Purpose Driven

Administration is the aspect of ministry that many pastors love
to hate. Among the many pastoral duties, administration consumes
the largest amount of time — 40 percent. Yet, according to studies,
pastors dislike administration more than any other task.

Sometimes I hear a fellow pastor say in frustration, "I hate
administration!" or "I hate management!" Usually one of two reasons follows.

The first is, "It keeps me from people. I want more time with
people and less time with administration."

The second is, "It keeps me from doing what I'm really supposed to be doing as a minister."

I understand the feelings behind these statements, but I have come to view administration in precisely the opposite way.

Administration does not keep me from people. It *is* people. It doesn't prevent my serving them; it gives me a way to serve them. Designing the bulletin, for example, is not simply completing a duty; it is designing the bulletin to enable people to worship God. Every administrative task, no matter how routine, is based in helping people.

Nor does administration detract me from my purpose. As a pastoral leader, my purpose is to enable this church, this particular group of God's people, to fulfill its mission. How can I help people fulfill their God-given mission apart from administration?

Management can be perceived as a binding activity or a freeing one. It can be viewed as hindering the mission or helping to fulfill it. Management becomes a positive thing when it is people centered and purpose driven.

Keeping It People Centered

Virtually all management issues deal with people. At our Monday staff meeting, for example, perhaps 75 percent of the time is spent talking about individuals. The staff discusses, "What are their gifts? How can we minister to them? How do we keep them from burning out? How do we discipline them?" One person could say that sitting in a meeting for two and a half hours is administrative work. But another person could say that the same meeting is spent planning for the spiritual growth of people. Both people are right.

Managing is ministering to people. In fact, it's difficult to think of any administrative duty that is not people centered.

Every Sunday, for example, people who attend Wooddale Church register their attendance. On the back of the registration cards, many write comments or questions about the service or church. Every question receives a response from me or another pastor, either in writing or by phone. That requires a lot of time holding a dictation machine. That could be perceived as administration, but I prefer to consider that as teaching, an opportunity to instruct people on why we worship as we do. I don't see that as significantly different from a hospital call or visiting someone's home.

Some people say, "I hate going to committee meetings. There aren't going to be any committee meetings in heaven." In response, we should ask, "What are committee meetings?" They are people getting together around a task. There are going to be many things like that in heaven.

The elders at Wooddale Church tell me repeatedly that a highlight of their month is the board meeting. Why? Because the other elders support them and pray for them. Together the elders conduct the business of the church, but they love their time together. Sometimes it is hard to get them to leave the meetings.

Management is not simply pushing papers. It is ministering to people.

Keeping It Purpose Driven

Readers of *In Search of Excellence* learned a lot about 3M. One reason 3M is Minnesota's premier corporation and an industry leader is that it has a tight, dominant corporate philosophy. Peters and Waterman wrote that 3M operates under a clearly stated purpose that makes the company what it is. But beyond these basics, the managers allow a great deal of entrepreneurial freedom.

At Wooddale Church we have tried to reproduce that same strong sense of purpose and freedom. We repeat the purpose of the church in documents, in church services, and in groups and classes. The purpose of this congregation can be summarized in one sentence: "The purpose of Wooddale Church is to honor God by bringing lives into harmony with him and one another through fellowship, discipleship, and evangelism." The church is structured to fulfill this purpose. We have boards for fellowship, discipleship, and evangelism. Each year we hold three weeks of special activities: one for fellowship, one for discipleship, and one for evangelism.

Beyond this central purpose, we grant freedom. For example,

Wooddale's adult congregations (which are like adult Sunday school classes) vary greatly. Each can choose its own social events or the amount of teaching time during a session. The board of elders does approve the teachers of these congregations, but the character and practice of each group are shaped by the group members themselves. This freedom, which lay people appreciate, does not work against the succinct congregational purpose. Rather, it wouldn't be possible without it.

A clear church purpose also gives direction and momentum to pastors. Many pastors are driven not by a purpose but by preaching, based on the old notion that people are called to preach. But as a pastor, I am not called just to preach. I am called to help this church fulfill its God-given mission. If that mission requires that I preach, I will preach. If it requires me to do something else, I will do something else. Knowing the mission and purpose of this congregation helps me to determine where to invest my energies.

What does it take to develop a people-centered, purpose-driven congregation?

Here are several suggestions, clustered in two broad responsibilities: (1) concentrate on critical tasks, and (2) streamline structures.

Concentrate on Critical Tasks

Several elements are involved when we concentrate on the critical tasks.

• *Communicate the philosophical base.* People need to understand the premises from which the church is operating. They want to know why the church is doing what it is doing. That takes consistent communication over a period of time.

One of the wisest things we have done at Wooddale was to develop a six-week course in leadership. A leading lay person, Austin Chapman, and I taught the course to groups of ten to twelve people selected for their leadership ability or potential. Every six weeks we invited a new group and taught the course again. After a couple of years, virtually every leader or potential leader in the church understood why we were doing what we were doing. They had read the same books and now approached congregational leadership with some common assumptions. From this base, the leaders have been able to make better decisions and earn trust from the congregation.

● *Put the best people in the areas of highest priority.* The immediate needs of a congregation do not remain static. During the early years of a pastor's tenure, a great deal of energy may be spent in recruiting staff or developing structures. Those tasks monopolize time for a while. Once they are complete, or when needs change, completely different priorities may emerge. The role of the pastor is to identify the immediate priorities and place the most competent people there.

The place for a congregation's best people is not necessarily on the governing board of the church. It is wherever the most pressing priority of the church lies. When a church has a small board and lean structure, people can be moved to where they are most needed. When they understand that the task is a high priority of the church and uses their gifts, they love serving in this way.

One of Wooddale's most competent leaders, for example, doesn't hold any position. We realized Wooddale had a responsibility to serve as a teaching congregation to other churches interested in growth, so I asked him to develop a program for that. He did. Then our music minister, though gifted musically, needed assistance in creating a strategic plan for music staffing and education. This same lay leader headed that project. Currently Wooddale is considering planting a church, and he is involved in planning for that. The church benefits by having this person free to move to critical areas, and frankly, he enjoys it.

● *Allow people to remain in areas that utilize their gifts.* Many churches do not allow someone to serve in one position for more than three years in a row. The practice is designed to protect the organization from bad leaders, but often it has the effect of taking people who have good judgment and removing them from positions of leadership so they can no longer exercise their gifts. If people are gifted in leadership, why prevent them from using that gift? We have drafted a compromise that allows elders to serve consecutive two-year terms for up to ten years. The church is only helped when people are allowed to serve in ways that utilize their strengths.

• *Listen to people and use their complaints.* 3M is known world-wide for its innovative research and development, which has led to products such as Post-it Notes. What is the number-one source of ideas for new products for 3M? A team of brilliant product engineers?

No. Customer complaints.

Would that churches would emulate that technique and use complaints constructively rather than get defensive. Complaints at Wooddale have proven a good source of ideas. For example, people complained about clogged parking lots, so we put up signs that say you must turn left when you drive out of the lot. A simple change, but it has made Sunday morning more enjoyable for many people.

When the final plans for our second building were presented to the congregation at a business meeting, somebody said, "If you're downstairs, it's a long way to get to the stairwell. Why don't we put in another stairwell?" We could have ignored the complaint. After all, the plans had been drafted by excellent architects and reviewed and commented on previously. But it was a great idea, so we told the architect to draw in another stairwell. Now that the building is constructed, we realize that it never would have worked without that stairwell. One of the manager's tasks is to listen to people and try to use those comments constructively.

Streamline Structures

In addition to concentrating on critical tasks, streamlining structures also helps us stay people centered and purpose driven. Here are the principles we use to keep structures sleek.

• *Subordinate structure to action.* It doesn't take much organization to run a church. Yet frequently I talk to people in churches that literally have more positions than people to fill them. That doesn't make sense. There is no value in organization for organization's sake. I disagree with the approach of getting people into the church by putting them on a committee or into a job. I think that's an anti-ministry philosophy.

What the church needs is for people to be involved in ministry. Whatever structures will enable that are needed, but beyond those, organization only hinders. We need lean structures that focus on action, that free people for ministry. We tell people repeatedly that ministry is more important than being on a board or committee, even when that board is making decisions about your area of ministry.

A few years ago a young executive in the church came to me and said, "I was approached to be on the evangelism board. What do you think I should do?"

She clearly had the gift of evangelism. She was bringing more people to the Lord and to the church than perhaps anybody else at that time. I said to her, "Kathy, it would be absurd for you to sit in board meetings when what you're good at is winning people to Jesus Christ." She was relieved to hear that she didn't have to give up evangelism to join the evangelism committee.

● *Use task forces rather than committees.* A task force keeps structures lean because it disbands when its task has been accomplished. Standing committees, on the other hand, continue whether or not there is a pressing need for them. When a task force is established, it is given a single purpose, budget, and deadline. We tell people, "Your task is to solve the parking shortage by May 1." Or, "Your mission is to find someone for this position by the end of the year." When that mission is completed, the task force disbands, and its members are free to move to other areas of need.

● *Select accomplishers rather than representatives.* I attended a conference given by the American Management Association where one speaker made a significant point about college trustees. "When you pick trustees or regents for a college or university," the speaker said, "there is only one characteristic you are looking for: good judgment. You are not looking for people who are rich or people who are powerful; if they have money and power and bad judgment, they'll ruin the institution. But if they have good judgment, they'll figure out a way to get the money and the power."

A similar principle applies when selecting people for boards or committees. In members of a pastoral search committee, for example, what qualities are needed? Really, only one: competence to find a new senior pastor. But often churches select people for such a task force based on representation. The church looks for someone old, someone young; a male, a female; a black, a white; someone rich, someone poor; a newcomer, and an oldtimer. But the group could consist solely of 18-year-old women if each possessed the judgment needed to select a new pastor. What counts is the ability to get the job done, and appointments should be made accordingly.

● *Avoid "leadership only" positions.* Committees become more effective and realistic when they are involved in implementing the decisions they make. Few things are worse, for example, than a Christian education committee's making decisions about the Sunday school and handing them to the actual teachers. When CE committee members also teach a Sunday school class, they make better decisions, because they must carry out the decisions made. In short, nobody's ministry should be exclusively in governance.

● *Limit the size of decision-making bodies.* Many churches, especially large ones, have boards that are quite large, sometimes with as many as twenty-five people. The rationale is, "We need a larger board because we have a larger church, and we want to be more representative." But a larger board is not more representative; it is less representative.

In reality, the maximum number of people that ought to be in a decision-making group is approximately eight or ten. Once a group gets larger than that, it develops, formally or informally, an executive committee of two or three people. So groups larger than ten don't distribute the decision; they restrict it to two or three.

● *Create "linking pins" in the church organization.* A large church in the East had two boards with parallel power but no link between them. The deacons had the power to call a staff member, and the trustees had the power to fund the position. Eventually, the deacons unanimously called someone as youth pastor, but the trustees unanimously refused to pay his salary. There was no choice, then, but to go to the congregation, which was immediately polarized because it had to choose between two groups of leaders.

Because of painful scenarios such as these, it is wise to provide "linking pins" throughout the organizational structure. A linking pin is someone who serves to connect two groups. At Wooddale, for example, the senior pastor is the linking pin between the board of elders and the pastoral staff. He serves as a member of both groups and can interpret the concerns of one to the other. The trustee board chairman is also an elder. The chair of a trustee board subcommittee is also a member of the trustee board. In this way, no part of the organization operates independently of the rest.

 ● *Keep the constitution accurate and flexible.* The constitution can play an important and positive role by clarifying policy. The pastor ought to master the constitution and become expert in the rules that govern the life of the church.

I am committed to playing by the rules embodied in the constitution. For example, when I came to Wooddale, the constitution stated that everyone must abide by the terms of the church covenant, which included abstinence from the sale and use of alcoholic beverages. Several leaders realized this provision hindered the congregation from reaching people who needed Christ but chose to drink in moderation. But the congregation lived by that rule until they later voted to change it.

Constitutions need to reflect accurately the beliefs and practices of the church — and be changed if they don't. After our annual meeting last February, I said to one person, "We really goofed this year because we didn't change the constitution."

She responded, "How could you possibly change the constitution? There's nothing left to change."

I said, "Then it must be time to start changing it back to the way it used to be." A constitution is not a static document, but a dynamic one that reflects the changes in the organization. Then it can clarify procedures for a congregation and minimize confusion.

Many churches do not regard the constitution as dynamic, of course, and they resist changes to it. Even in those situations, a pastor can do things to make the document less restrictive. One way is to use terms like *normally*. For example, our constitution says that we will have worship services every Sunday. No church in Minnesota has worship services every Sunday, because on a few Sundays every year snow makes it impossible to get to church. Technically, canceling worship would be breaking the provisions of the constitution. So we have changed our constitution to say "We will normally have worship every Sunday" and thus have provided for the exception to the rule.

Another way to take the constitution seriously and still be able to react to changing church life is to establish groups for handling unusual circumstances. Our constitution has spending limits. But suppose a missionary calls us and says, "I have a member of my family who is critically ill; we need to charter a jet ambulance and get her out of this country within the next four hours, or she will die. We need fifteen thousand dollars." To fulfill the request might involve breaking the rules of the constitution. So we established a crisis-management team, people of good judgment who will decide such cases.

The Challenge of Change

While helping a church become more people centered and purpose driven, a pastor will encounter several obstacles.

One is people's natural resistance to change. Change, even positive change, creates stress. When a church goes from an inadequate to a wonderful building, for example, there is still the pain of leaving behind the old building, even though the move is a positive and a good thing. And change comes more slowly for churches that do not have a tradition of change.

A second obstacle is that many pastors have not had positive administrative models. They know how to preach, but they have not had as much exposure to, or experience in, church management. We all tend to dislike things we don't know how to do well. The first few times I traveled overseas, for example, were unpleasant, because I didn't know where to check in or how to get my seat assignment. But once those elements are figured out, travel becomes more enjoyable. Similarly, administration becomes more enjoyable as we develop experience in it.

A third obstacle to a people-centered, purpose-driven ministry is lack of time in a congregation. In my early days at Wooddale, I requested a baptismal robe that cost approximately seventy dollars. My request was turned down. Twelve or thirteen years later, however, when Wooddale was in the midst of a building program, a custodian pointed out to me that the design of the platform would put a large gulf between me and the congregation. I called the vice-chairman of the building committee and said, "I am not willing to preach with all the instruments and musicians between me and the people." The plan had been approved, and the concrete had been poured, but he said, "Fine." The plans were changed.

A dozen years before I couldn't get a seventy-dollar baptismal robe, and now, while a building was partially constructed, they were willing to change it. That's because they have grown to trust me. The manager of any organization needs to understand that it takes time to win authority that allows for significant change.

People Centered and Purpose Driven

Sometimes people ask, "Should the church be run like a business?"

The answer is that the church ought to be run correctly — with a commitment to people and a passion to fulfill the church's mission. Then people will learn in the church how to run their businesses.

One Sunday night I got a telephone call from a church member who works at Honeywell Corporation.

"I'm going into a job interview for a higher management position," he said, "and here are some of the questions I'm going to be asked. Everything I know about management is what I've been taught at church. How would you answer those questions at Wooddale? That's the way I want to answer the questions at Honeywell."

I was gratified to realize he felt the church had taught him something about organizational life.

Administration does not have to be perceived as a drain on ministry. Rather, once the church's primary mission is established, management is essential to free the church to fulfill that purpose.

PART TWO
The Tasks

In church management, sometimes pastors follow directives. But we also motivate people, set goals, organize, and initiate. To put it another way, a good pastor-administrator is a good leader.

— Arthur DeKruyter

CHAPTER FOUR

The Many Sides of Administration

Early in my ministry, I attended a social gathering in an elder's home. I had just begun thinking about the importance of the pastor's administrative role, and during the evening's conversation, I expressed some of my ideas.

The elder, who happened to be a sharp businessman and a good manager, temporarily forgot most of his own rules for dealing with people. "Never forget that you're working *for* the church," he informed me in the presence of his peers and mine. "Your job is to carry out the church's directives. Remember, we're paying your salary."

I still feel the sting of those words.

As time passed, however, I noticed that the churches accomplishing things were led by pastors who were, in fact, good administrators — they followed the will of the people, but they also helped shape the church. Harold Ockenga's ministry at Park Street Church in Boston, for example, left a deep impression on me.

At Christ Church of Oak Brook, the board makes policy and the pastor administers it. That means the pastor has the responsibility to implement programs, but also the freedom to lead the board into new policy decisions.

To master church management, one must master administration. It is vital, then, to be clear about the full dimensions of administration. Most pastors recognize they, as administrators, are responsible to carry out board policy. But some are less clear about how an administrator also leads.

In chapter 1, Don Cousins has shown briefly that managers are leaders. Let me, in this chapter, explore the many sides of pastoral administration.

An Administrator Appeals to Higher Needs

Whether I'm creating or implementing a program, people need to be motivated to support it with their time, talents, and treasures. Motivating them is my job as administrator.

Some preachers try to motivate by harping: "If you don't do this, you will one day be responsible before God, your judge." But that doesn't work in our congregation.

Instead, I find Maslow's hierarchy of needs helps me understand human drives and ambitions, and consequently, helps me motivate people. I try to appeal to the higher needs on Maslow's chart — self-fulfillment and service to God and others. When I address those needs, people automatically become motivated, provide funds for church programs, and follow enthusiastically.

For example, we constructed our church building because of one of these higher needs. Eighty families were packed into a gymnasium for worship services. Children overflowed from available classrooms. We needed a home, yes. But more important, with our own building, we could establish ourselves as a dynamic presence in the Oak Brook community. Our motivation compelled us beyond the basic need of adequate shelter. We wanted to make a bold statement for our Lord.

The result is a warm, spacious building on a main thoroughfare. We committed ourselves to a high mortgage, but today every one of our members would confirm it was worth it.

An Administrator Talks in Pictures

The pastor may be able to appeal to the congregation's higher needs but sometimes still cannot convince people to act or give. Often the problem is not lack of vision as much as a lack of a mental picture. People are unable to picture a solution to a need.

Consequently, I try to dramatize solutions. For instance, we spurred the vision for our new building by unveiling a beautiful scale model. We displayed it in a bank, a restaurant, and the lobby of a local hotel. We committed ourselves publicly, and our members rose to the challenge of establishing the dream.

Our members have been inspired to participate in many other projects because they were excited by a picture of what could be accomplished: "*Imagine* sending a busload of youngsters on excursions throughout the United States!" "*Imagine* our facilities as a focal point for religious music in the area!"

A few years ago we heard about Christian villagers who lived along the northern border of India. One of their most pressing needs was for church buildings. We were impressed and sought to help. I began by giving our congregation a picture: small churches in villages, each a little "Christ Church of Such-and-Such a Village." We visualized these villagers going to church on Sunday morning, worshiping in a different culture, but worshiping the same Lord. "Wouldn't it be great," I asked, "if they could worship in a building? Why don't we help them get a building?" And before we knew it, we had done just that.

Effective motivators talk in figurative language rather than in abstract detail. Jack Kennedy didn't talk about spending money on "space exploration," but about "putting a man on the moon in ten years." That picture caught our imagination and motivated an entire nation.

Likewise, those who direct the ministries of the church find themselves charged with enlarging people's vision. And vision comes from picturing what God wants to do.

An Administrator Pursues Goals — Prudently

Have you seen any preachers carrying donkeys lately? They often do, you know.

They're like the old man in the fable who was traveling with a child and a donkey. As they passed through the first village, the man led the donkey and the child walked behind. The villagers said the old man was a fool for not riding his sturdy beast of burden. So he climbed on, seeking to please the crowd.

In a second village, people said the old man was cruel to the child, making him walk while enjoying the ride himself. So the man got off and put the child on the animal's back.

In the third village, the consensus was that the child was lazy because he was forcing the old man to walk. So they *both* rode.

In a fourth village, the bystanders said the poor donkey was overworked. The man was last seen carrying the donkey down the road.

It's important to listen to the will of the people, but it can get out of hand. Crowds can be fickle. That's why I firmly believe the pastor-administrator should set goals for the church. That's not to say we stay aloof from our people. We pastors must dream dreams and set goals for the church, but we shouldn't be afraid to dream with people around us, nor to set goals in conjunction with the board. Napoleon Hill calls this a "brain trust." When two people think together, their thoughts somehow combine into ideas bigger than both of them. The wise administrator will take the initiative to set goals, but never form those goals in solitude.

The seeds of dynamic goals are nurtured during personal

meditation and prayer. In the rush of activity, I mustn't forget to listen quietly to God.

But next, a good administrator outlines these goals and shows them to the right people. As any pastor knows, not all the people with power are elected officers. But in office or out, the informal executive board — the individuals the congregation follows — should be consulted.

I learned a valuable lesson about this in a church that had two bright orange doors in the front of an otherwise dignified sanctuary.

"Why are the doors painted orange?" I asked the elected leaders.

"Pastor, you'd better talk to the fellow who painted them."

"I don't think that's a liturgical color," I remarked. "In fact, I think we should repaint them."

"You'd better talk to the man who painted them," was the nervous reply. So I did.

It turned out the painter had been hired by a wealthy immigrant who loved the Dutch hero William of Orange. He had paid for the painting of the church sanctuary out of his own pocket.

I finally got the doors repainted, but it was far more difficult than I estimated, even though many people agreed the color was atrocious.

Some powerful people are easily threatened and can shatter the dreams we are working to build. Others enjoy knocking down our plans as a matter of course. Others still, whether officers or not, are looked to by members for insight; their opinions matter to many people. So, we need to contact this core group first when important goals are being set. With some honest and skillful human-relations work, we can shape our goals better, avoid unnecessary conflict, and gain vital support. Only after endorsements from people in this core group do we show the goals to the entire congregation.

At the same time, you cannot bypass the elected governing board, as I discovered long ago, to my regret.

In my first congregation, I felt we needed to reorganize the structure of the church. So I talked to a couple of talented business-men in the congregation who were known for their organizational expertise. They analyzed our structure, pointed out its weakness, and suggested a new approach. They did a superb job. It couldn't be faulted.

The problem was I had bypassed the governing board, and before we could move on the plan, the board had to approve it. They had not authorized the study, nor had they been consulted during the process. When the plan was explained to them, they wouldn't even talk about it.

"Since this was all done outside the board and without our knowledge and approval, we don't even recognize it," they said. "Officially it doesn't exist." When I suggested we start over, this time with them taking the initiative, they refused. By that time, I had embittered them.

I had made use of the movers and shakers but to no avail; I hadn't gone through official channels. A prudent administrator does both.

An Administrator Sets Worthy Goals

Big goals normally excite a church and win congregational support faster than small goals. Denominations sometimes make the mistake of trying to start churches by erecting small buildings and then sending someone to fill them with people. Unfortunately, the denomination has announced to the community that its vision is small. Highly motivated people are attracted by great ideas. When we limit vision, we immediately cut off those who have the capacity to catch a broad, exciting vision for ministry.

One of our members wanted to serve Christ, but he told me he didn't want to organize or lead any more meetings in the church; he'd had enough of that. I thought about it for a few days and came back with a suggestion. "Why not start a community breakfast or lunch? A monthly meeting over breakfast, for example, might at-tract business people who commute to Chicago. Nationally known speakers could address them on relevant topics. Periodically we can bring in an inspirational speaker, and I could lead with prayer. This community is growing and it lacks cohesiveness. It would be a way our church could serve the community."

That caught his interest. So we started the Executive Breakfast Club of Oak Brook, now the biggest club of its type in the Chicago area. Average attendance is about five hundred, although we've had up to twelve hundred people attend. We have had speakers like Gerald Ford as well as business people who talk about their faith. We've had people converted to Christ. Many people come to the church because of it.

Here was a man who was tired of routine ministry, but who was actually just underemployed. He was energized by the vision of doing something big for Christ in the community.

Naturally, I don't believe good things only come in large packages. Many people *are* served best in smaller ways. People have left our church because they felt it grew too large for them, and I respect that. But even a small church lifts up a large vision to its members, albeit in a different way. To be an intimate, caring church family, for example, is hardly a small vision.

The Administrator Works Backwards

It's easy to find a path through a maze if you start at the end and work *backwards* to the starting point. Most children who spend much time with puzzle books know that.

An administrator determines the steps to be taken to reach a goal. A *good* administrator establishes the goals for a congregation and then works backwards to develop a path to reach those goals.

A friend asked if I would meet with his church's planning board. This small Episcopal congregation had twin goals: to build new facilities and to develop a large youth ministry. Their present youth program was small, but they thought including a special youth facility in their building plans would help it grow.

After some discussion, I realized they were planning a youth building but weren't considering how to nurture a large youth program. Working backwards in our planning, we realized the building could happen only after they hired a youth worker who could build a strong program. Only then could they dream realistically about having a youth building. Then, a larger youth program would necessitate the expansion of their facilities. That, in fact, is what happened.

A few years ago, I felt we needed a healing service. I knew my congregation, however. Many would be skeptical, equating a healing service with flamboyant faith-healers, which would not be the type of service our church could appreciate.

So I worked backwards with them for the next several months. I showed them the need that would be fulfilled, both from a biblical and pastoral perspective. We talked about the different healings that people would experience, emotional and psychological as well as physical. We talked about the liturgy that could be used and the tone of the service it would set.

Once they clearly saw the goal, the end of the process, they were willing and able to take the steps necessary to get there. Now our monthly healing service is one they wouldn't do without.

An Administrator Thinks about Vital Details

When I was a boy, my family owned a retail hardware store. That's where I learned the nuts and bolts of business. I learned to pay attention to little things, and I saw the problems that resulted when I didn't.

Many aspects of church work are as mundane as nuts, bolts, sink fixtures, and set screws. But you can't ignore them.

A few years ago, we began two morning worship services, and the increased traffic was too much for a parking lot designed for simpler days. Things never reached a critical point. Our members grumbled a bit, but little more. No trustee received a flash of inspiration that said, "Do something about this!" We limped along, not coming to grips with the situation.

As an administrator with an eye for detail, I began to see the growing problem. I had to get involved in additional details — talking about the legitimate need for a new lot and motivating the church and board to make some changes. An attention to vital detail — the growing irritation over finding a parking space — made the difference.

Lacking that attention, things may have continued unchanged for a long time, and a subtle message would have gone out to our community: *Christ Church has grown to the point it can't handle any more people.*

An Administrator Leads

In church management, pastor-administrators do all sorts of things. Sometimes we follow directives. But we also motivate people, set goals, organize, and initiate. To put it another way, a good administrator is a good leader.

So I try not to confine my image of administration, as did the elder I mentioned at the beginning of the chapter. Nor would I say a pastor should remain aloof and lead only from the pulpit. Instead, pastors can do anything and everything that helps the church flourish and reach out to its neighbors in the name of Christ. That will happen when we recognize the many aspects of effective church administration.

It is enormously important which direction people are looking. But how can we move from looking backward to looking forward?

— Leith Anderson

CHAPTER FIVE

Looking to the Future

As soon as people walk into a church, they can tell if it is oriented toward the past or the future. They don't discover that by what they see as much as by what they *hear*. When I visit a church or catch conversations in my congregation, I listen to how people talk about one subject: the greatest days of the church.

At one well-known midwestern church, for example, visitors may hear people say: "I remember when folks lined up to get into evening services. Conventions of major national associations were held here. When people came to town, they attended here." Their glory days are past, not future. The result, for both the listeners and people speaking, is an overwhelming feeling of sadness.

When I came to Wooddale Church, people spoke similarly: "I remember when we used to. . . . I remember when attendance was growing instead of declining." I found it emotionally difficult to be involved in conversations in which people quoted somebody else's sermon, said the music or the ushering was better before I came, or pointed out that this week's attendance was lower than the previous week's.

I knew, as every pastor does, that it is enormously important which direction the people are looking. But how could we move from looking backward to looking forward? How could I shift people's wistful gaze at the past to an expectant peering into the future?

The God Who Transcends Time

It takes a great deal of faith and courage for a pastor to switch the direction people look. It demands waiting it out and working it out. There is not one simple answer.

But the starting point for any answer lies in God. Vision is rooted in God. God transcends time: He is the God of the past, but repeatedly in Scripture he is the God of the future. We need to fix our attention on who he is and what he wants to do. We can't, therefore, live only in the past, because God is calling us *to* something. There's always something out in front of us.

Harry Truman visited Oliver Wendell Holmes, Jr., when Holmes was in his nineties. When Truman walked into the room, the retired justice was reading Plato's *Republic*. Truman asked him, "Mr. Justice, why at this point in life would you be reading something like that?"

Oliver Wendell Holmes, Jr., replied, "I may be old, but I haven't stopped growing."

If somebody can have that perspective about law and philosophy, ought we not all the more have that perspective about the church of Jesus Christ?

Eventually, this general vision of God's purposes for the local church needs to become specific: What mission has God given our particular congregation?

Too often that is immediately taken to be numerical growth. But for a church in the Iron Range of Minnesota, which has had in recent years as high as 80 percent unemployment, moderate decline can be success. On the other hand, Wooddale is located in a city that has grown from 24,000 to 34,000 in the last five years. If we weren't growing, it's hard to believe we would be fulfilling all of our mission given by God.

In either case, though, the appropriate specific mission grows out of the knowledge that God is leading his people into the future.

Present Needs, Not Past Success

What causes a church to settle into past-directed thinking is not so much present difficulty as past success. Churches don't longingly remember defeats and conflicts; they grow nostalgic over past victories and expansions. Past success can become a staggering weight. What, people wonder, can they possibly do to surpass those days?

A similar dynamic occurs for any person successful early in life. Consider Jonas Salk, whose pioneering medical research led to the development of a vaccine for polio. His achievement immortalized him. What possibly could he do next?

Recently, however, Jonas Salk is in the news again — not because of polio, but because of AIDS. He's working on a vaccine. Here is a person who said, *Yes, I've had past success. But there are needs in the present.* He's using the skills he has developed to help his present generation.

In a similar way, a church lifts the burden of past success when it focuses instead on present needs: What do the people in this community and world need? How can we provide that?

At Wooddale, probably 99 percent of the people would now say the greatest days of the church are ahead, because they see present needs they can help meet.

One man who led our junior high program became a missionary to the Sundanese. Of the thirty million Sundanese in West Java, only one hundred are believers. Yet in this man's two and a half years of ministry there, fourteen more have come to Christ. It's phenomenal and almost unprecedented.

In a morning service he told the congregation, "This is not because I'm a great linguist; it's because you prayed." He read from letters he'd received from people in the church: "I pray every day." "I run five miles every morning, and as I run I pray for the Sundanese people." An 11-year-old had written, "I get down on my knees every night and pray for the Sundanese."

The people at Wooddale think that in the next ten years thirty million Sundanese are going to be won to Christ. They're not talking about yesterday; they're talking about tomorrow. Why? They have been gripped by the needs of these Sundanese. Past success fades in the light of present needs and opportunities.

A Few People of Vision

Most people are not persons of vision. In a church of hundreds or even thousands of members, a leader will probably find only a few.

Part of the reason is generational. The baby-boomer generation has, until now, been present oriented. The generation, as a whole, has given little concern to traditions or to the future. But foresight won't necessarily come from the older generation, either; the elderly may be more prone to look to the successes of the past.

Some leaders lament the paucity of people of vision. But to move forward, an institution requires only a few. Robert Kennedy put it this way in his great quote: "Some people look at the way things are and ask why; others look at the way things could be and ask why not." A church needs only a few such people — ideally, a pastor and one or two lay people. If they are leaders, others will follow.

Many pastors, serving a tradition-entrenched congregation, wonder how it can ever move forward: *There aren't enough people with vision. No one sees how things could be.* But usually there is one other person, or two, who can envision greatness, and gradually that influence can spread.

People with vision don't even have to be on the cutting edge of ecclesiastical innovation. The field of medicine provides an analogy. Most U.S. physicians are not researchers (and most hospitals are not teaching hospitals). Rather, most doctors treat patients on the basis of what they learn at seminars or read in journals.

Similarly, a few pastors and churches in the United States pioneer new structures, approaches to evangelism, and methods of outreach. But the vast majority minister on the basis of what they learn at seminars or read in journals. A church's few persons with vision may not be on the cutting edge, but if they are willing to learn, evaluate ideas, and adopt some of them, they can move the church forward.

The Pastor's Role: Looking Out the Window

What is the pastor's role in all this?

A few years ago a magazine ad pictured a man standing in his office, looking out the window. The caption read: "Why would a company pay this man $100,000 a year to look out the window?" The point: Every organization needs someone who looks out the window, outside the organization, to the world and to the future. A pastor helps the congregation by looking out the window.

But how much time ought a pastor devote to dreaming of the future, especially with a multitude of immediate concerns?

The answer varies with each situation, obviously, but much of the answer is determined by how long a pastor has been with the current congregation. Strangely, natural tendencies work against effective vision.

Typically, when pastors come to a church, they are not vested in the programs. Therefore, they can be objective: "We shouldn't be having this many services," or "We shouldn't be doing Vacation Bible School this way." Most pastors start with a burst of energy in envisioning how things could be. (In addition, when pastors come to a church, few members call or trust them with information. This frees time to look ahead.) But new ministers' ideas often are not readily accepted by the people. Even a good vision can die because people haven't yet learned to trust the pastor.

But after pastors have been in a church five or ten years, most programs reflect their ideas or bear their imprimatur. Their schedules are jammed, so they have little time to dream about the future. Momentum shifts to maintaining the programs they have built.

We need to reverse the process.

When we start in a congregation, most of our time should be devoted to current program, not looking ahead. Then, gradually, we need to slide the scale until we spend more time on future projects. Why? Because a congregation won't follow a pastor in looking forward unless it trusts that pastor, and building trust takes time.

I know one pastor who went to a church that was ready to build, change its constitution, and reach out. He accomplished more in his first year than I accomplished in my first seven or eight. But that doesn't happen often.

Most pastors enter situations in which people remember the past, and problems exist. These pastors have to build credibility. The best way is to concentrate on existing programs. As a pastor works hard inside the given structures, the congregation develops the trust that later allows the pastor to lead people forward.

It's taken a quarter of my life to reach this point, but now, many weeks I am able to spend more time on future possibilities than on current program. This week, for example, I have concentrated on a variety of dreams: starting a daughter church, providing a Saturday night service, expanding staff, and helping new missions projects. Now, these are fitting tasks, but they probably would not have been when I began at Wooddale.

Pastors need to look out the window, although in the early years it pays to spend more time at the desk.

Obstacles to the Pastor's Role

Every pastor would like more time to look out the window.

But that requires overcoming significant obstacles.

First, we hands-on types may find looking forward painful, because there is so much present work demanding attention. A more hidden, formidable obstacle is our need for affirmation. Planning doesn't receive much recognition, at least not nearly as much as direct ministry does.

When I devoted most of my time to hands-on ministry, I could see my impact. When a baby was born, the parents called me, often before they called the grandparents. When someone was dying, I would spend a whole night at the hospital. When the family made decisions about shutting off respirators, I watched the switch being thrown.

Because of the congregation's growth, however, we may have three or four babies born in one week. I can't be there for them all. In order to fulfill our mission, I have to make sure somebody will be there, but it can't always be me. My role increasingly is to look ahead for the entire body — to look out the window — and that means I have to give up many wonderful strokes from hands-on ministry.

Having said that, however, every pastor must give direct, hands-on attention to some areas. Which ones? The few most essential for the congregation right now.

Recently, for example, our staff discussed the prayer life of Wooddale Church. Although there is much prayer in various cells and subcongregations, I'm convinced, by my own observation, that the vast majority of that prayer is for personal needs. People are praying earnestly for kids struggling with drugs and adults fighting cancer. But I sense we are not doing as well in praying for the fulfillment of our mission, for the services of the church, and for missions.

So the question came up: Who will lead the midweek prayer meeting that draws only a handful of people? I volunteered. I thought, *If I stop people in the hallway and ask "Will you pray with me on Wednesday night?" they are likely to come.* Our congregation won't move forward without corporate prayer, so right now I'm giving it hands-on attention.

Specific Strategies

It is not enough, of course, to look ahead in a general sense. Vision must translate into specific strategies:

● *Have people think next year, not this year.* At the start of school, Greg Weisman, our minister to junior high students, has planned his program for the entire school year. He has in print every time the group will play miniature golf. He knows when and where they will hold retreats, who the retreat speakers are, and which bus is scheduled. With the program completely planned, what's left for Greg to do?

Minister to kids.

He doesn't have to worry about a topic for next Sunday's lesson. He doesn't have to reserve the bus. He doesn't have to schedule a camp for the junior high Breakaway. Living week to week consumes energies for ministry. It is painful not to know what you're going to do next week. But planning ahead releases ministry, and that moves a congregation forward.

Further, as members see the pastor planning, they do the same. That spirit permeates the organization. Wooddale's treasurer, for example, doesn't sign checks. He looks at how we're going to fulfill the purpose of the church financially through 1992. He concentrates on modeling projected income, expenses, and debt service. That way, when an opportunity appears on the horizon, we know in what ways we're able to respond.

● *Spend time as a cultural anthropologist.* Pastors benefit from keeping their ear to the ground of culture. For example, one shift I failed to foresee is that people increasingly choose not to be classified by marital status. Whether they are single, divorced, separated — it's irrelevant to them, or at least they don't see that as a primary point of identification. Traditional categories — single and married — have become fuzzy because there are so many new classifications: living together, once divorced, separated but acting like a single, and others.

By listening for these rumblings, pastors can be ready for the eruption. We are asking serious questions: Is it time to reorganize singles ministry? Should we group according to preferred learning style? Or solely by age? Or more likely, should we group people by the age of their children? Already, we have placed no restrictions on which Sunday school class someone attends, and many singles attend classes composed primarily of couples.

In an increasingly pluralistic society, it's wise to offer options. (If I had my way, I'd lead one service in a sweatshirt, a second service in a suit, and a third service in a robe.) Baby boomers are highly tolerant of pluralism and comfortable with diversity. By studying culture — through seminars, books, and conversations — we can provide options when they're needed.

● *Plan for opportunities rather than problems.* This principle, advocated by Peter Drucker, helped the congregation about ten years ago, when we were ready to add a staff member. The choice narrowed to either a minister for counseling or a pastor of singles. The church couldn't afford both. Which position would most directly fulfill Wooddale's mission?

When we looked at projections for the area's singles population, we were stunned. The number of singles was going to increase rapidly. We said, "That's where the opportunity is. Many Christian counselors exist in the region, but who is going to seize this opportunity for singles?" We hired a pastor of singles.

Related to this is the well-recognized principle that a church staffs to grow, not because of growth. If the church-growth experts are right that a typical congregation should have one pastor for every 150 parishioners, then the time to add the second pastor is when the congregation reaches 151, not 300.

● *Emphasize ministry rather than structure.* Right now we are building a new sanctuary. We have planned for it for years, and we can't wait until it's completed. But when I want to upset people, I talk about "when it's time to sell this building and move." The idea stuns them, but it makes the point wonderfully: I am not beholden to this building. If in five or ten years this building doesn't fit the ministry God has called Wooddale to, we should tear it down. It is ministry we're concerned about. As we emphasize that, people are better able to let go of structure and move ahead.

Becoming Purpose Driven

I don't think of myself as a futurist. As I mentioned in Chapter 3, I prefer to think of myself as "purpose driven." Looking to the future is part of that. But being future oriented is not the end; it is only one means to the end of fulfilling Wooddale's congregational mission: "to honor God by bringing lives into harmony with him and one another."

Consider, for example, if the United States were to have a depression or nuclear disaster. There may not be any future, or at least only a painfully difficult one. To fulfill the purpose God has given us, we might be setting up bread lines or providing help for people with radiation burns. But that would be looking forward, with purpose.

Mother Teresa is future oriented, even though many of the street people she touches are going to die. But she is driven by a purpose. She is doing what's necessary to live as Jesus Christ would in the streets of Calcutta.

Karl Barth says that Christians are to be the "provisional representatives of a new race." Would that all our churches were driven by that wonderful concept. We are provisional in the sense that we haven't arrived, but we are called to live as a new race of believers.

We are a future-oriented, purpose-driven people.

Most people prefer to skip the why questions and jump right into the how-to's. But a ministry philosophy is the key to working smart. Before we can form a workable strategy, we need to ask two questions: What do we know about the target group? What do we know about doing this ministry effectively?

— Don Cousins

CHAPTER SIX
Starting Ministries Successfully

Most ministers work hard. The question is: Do we also work *smart?*

In the marketplace, leaders are forced to work smart because the bottom line tells them if their strategies are working. But in ministry, the bottom line is less tangible. It's difficult to evaluate how well we're doing, so we tend to work hard, pray hard, and then just trust that the "bottom line" will turn out to God's liking.

Certainly we *should* work hard, pray diligently, and trust God. But we don't want to spin our wheels using unproductive strategies. The key is to be more specific about what we're trying to accomplish.

I was once part of a fine church youth group. The Bible was taught every week. The group served at a state hospital and a children's home. We sponsored activities on Friday, Saturday, and Sunday nights. There were Wednesday night Bible studies and Sunday morning classes. But the students were unenthused, and the group failed to grow. We had no end of activity, but it was unfocused and unproductive.

We began to wonder, *What would happen if we designed the program specifically to draw newcomers?*

So we built a program around outreach. Once a week we invited students to an evening of sports competition, contemporary Christian music, drama, multimedia, and a simple message from the Bible. The first night 150 students showed up; the Christians all had brought friends whom they'd been afraid to invite to our earlier activities designed just for believers. I brought three myself, and they came back the following week because they'd had such a positive experience. Many such friends became Christians, and the ministry continued to grow.

What happened? Did we work harder than other youth ministries? Not necessarily. We simply employed a strategy.

Since that time I've helped develop and refine various ministries at Willow Creek Community Church. The following steps, we've found, are central to launching a ministry well.

Build on Leadership, Not Need

Ask most leaders on what basis they start a ministry, and they'll say, "We see a need, and we try to meet it."

While need is undoubtedly the seed that plants a ministry idea, we've found need alone is an insufficient foundation upon which to build a ministry. We need to start with leadership. Any endeavor that works seems to require a strong leader.

It's easy to cite examples in industry: Where would Chrysler be without Lee Iacocca? Or IBM without Tom Watson? And in athletics: Peter Ueberroth and the Los Angeles Olympics. Or, better yet, religion: When God decided to start a nation, he went to Abraham. When he wanted to reach out to the Gentile world, he knocked Saul off a horse. Every successful undertaking starts with a leader.

Yet what do we often do in our churches? Well, we have a need, so we round up a committee and . . .

Most pastors consider three options when confronted with a need. Let's say there's rumbling about the lack of a junior high program. What can be done?

First, the pastor can run a program personally. In most cases, that adds an eleventh hat to a person already struggling under the weight of ten. And perhaps the pastor has few qualifications and little passion for junior high ministry.

Second, the pastor can ask a staff member to take on the ministry. But often the CE director ends up doing children's ministry, junior high, high school, college, and singles, and none of them well. Why? Because it's humanly impossible to do a great job in five different ministries at once.

A third option is to turn to well-intentioned parents. That creates problems of capability and continuity. Are the parents trained? Do they know how to direct a program that will build kids' spiritual maturity? Will they be motivated to serve after their kids graduate?

When Willow Creek faced the need for a junior high ministry, we decided to take a different approach. We made the difficult decision to put the need on hold until we found a qualified leader who could make that ministry his or her speciality.

We went four years without a junior high ministry — no youth meetings, no Sunday school, nothing. Parents asked us what we were doing for junior high kids, and we had to gulp and say, "We're looking for a leader, but right now we can't meet your needs."

We took a lot of heat from parents when there was nothing for their kids, but we knew a first-rate ministry would require a specialized leader. Only if we had the right person, with the right gifts, doing what he or she did best — and only then — could we expect great results.

We looked high and low for qualified junior high leaders — volunteer or paid. The man who eventually became our key leader had proven himself as a lay leader in our high school ministry. Because he worked full-time in the marketplace, he had limited time to devote to ministry, but he agreed to organize a few special events for junior highers. Eventually he developed such a zeal for that age group that he quit his job and joined our staff. He has since built a tremendous junior high ministry.

We could have begun with three or four untried volunteers. But we're convinced it was worth the wait to find the right person and build the ministry properly. It's a lot harder to undo and redo a weak program than to build a quality program from scratch.

Settle on One Purpose

Once we've found the key leader, we assemble five or six individuals to brainstorm about the ministry. This "think tank" typically consists of the ministry leader, several other people with a passion and corresponding giftedness for that ministry, and one or two staff members or elders. We aim for a mix of people, though each must be good at analyzing and strategizing.

This group may gather for a one-day planning retreat, or meet regularly for several months. To plan Willow Creek's missions ministry, eight or nine of us met several hours a month for a year and between meetings did individual research.

Our evangelism think tank, on the other hand, met only twice before we began to implement some of the ideas. It all depends on the complexity of the proposed ministry.

Our first task is to determine the primary purpose of the ministry. Just as we like our leaders to shoulder only one major responsibility, so we want every program or meeting to have only one declared purpose. If we're able to accomplish more than that, we consider it whipped cream.

Think of a typical Sunday morning service. Many churches

attempt to equip believers, bring nonbelievers to Christ, encourage fellowship, foster communication, and worship faithfully — all in one hour! Can teachers edify believers and evangelize the lost at the same time?

At Willow Creek, we concluded that we couldn't; the two audiences are too different. So we decided our single purpose for our Sunday morning service was to reach the nonchurched. We make no apology for not doing anything else as long as we accomplish our primary objective. Christians visit our Sunday service and say, "It's not a worship service. I couldn't live on this."

We say, "You're right; worship isn't our purpose on Sunday. You should visit our Wednesday night believers' service."

So the think tank's job is to identify *one* objective for the ministry. We want each ministry to do one thing well, to meet one need initially through the leadership of one key person.

We've noticed that when we meet one need thoroughly, we attract people and resources that enable us to move on and meet another need. If we do a great job of evangelism, people come to know Christ, they're thankful for what's happening in their lives, and they start giving financially. That allows us to start other ministries. But if we never did the first step right, we wouldn't accumulate the people or resources necessary to go to step two.

Having a single focus also benefits workers by helping them gauge their effectiveness. Our food pantry has one purpose: to get food and clothing to people in need. If it does nothing else but provide those necessities, it's a success. So, every time a pantry volunteer receives a thank-you note saying, "I don't know what I'd do without you," we know the pantry is reaching its goal.

But suppose the workers sensed the unspoken goal of leading every pantry walk-in to the Lord. Frustration would run high unless many people were coming to Christ. We wouldn't attach that purpose to the pantry without making it clearly the primary purpose and then training the workers so they could be effective witnesses.

It happens that as a result of distributing food, people have heard the gospel and become Christians. We've also discovered financial needs and marriages falling apart, and sent people to appropriate counseling. But these are side benefits. They don't have to happen for the ministry to be considered a success.

Determine a Philosophy of Ministry

The think tank's second task is tougher: to establish a philosophy of ministry.

Most people prefer to skip the why questions and jump right into the how-to's. But a ministry philosophy is the key to working smart. Before we can form a workable strategy for accomplishing our single task, we need to ask two questions: *What do we know about the target group? What do we know about doing this ministry effectively?*

In thinking through evangelism for Willow Creek, we began by asking, "What do we know about the average unbeliever?" We agreed that he probably will not change his life and world-view in one hour. He doesn't know who God is: he thinks God's outdated, a rule maker, a killjoy, no fun. He's busy enough without church, and so on.

Then we asked, "What do we know about effective evangelism?" We decided it doesn't pressure people to change quickly, because that's unrealistic. It usually isn't as effective in a single event as through a continuing process. It helps people process truth systematically, so they can make a rational decision that will lead to long-term commitment.

This helped us circle in on the evangelistic approach that would be most effective at Willow Creek. We decided that our overall thrust in evangelism would be gradually to change unbelievers' concepts of God.

Suppose I said to you: "I want you to meet a friend of mine. But I have to warn you: he's hard to get along with. He's selfish; he talks a lot about himself; he's moody; and, oh yes, he probably won't have any money and will expect you to cover his expenses, so bring your wallet!" Would you want to meet him? Probably not.

But suppose I said, "You've got to meet my friend! He's been a true friend for more than ten years and would give me the shirt off his back. If I were in a jam, he'd drop everything to come to my side. He's the most gracious, giving, thoughtful person I've ever met. I could trust this guy with anything." Would you like to meet that person? Of course.

Unfortunately, most unbelievers see God more like my first friend than my second. That's why they've chosen to refuse or ignore him. Our job is to introduce them to the true God. If we can change their *understanding* of God, chances are we can change their *response* to God.

So, in everything we do as a church, every statement we make — whether through a clean, well-designed building, or through the music we use on Sunday, or the written material we make available — we make it clear that God and his followers are *not* backward or second-rate or dull. And each week we design a Sunday morning service that creatively presents the true identity of God and shatters unbelievers' misconceptions.

It takes time to formulate a philosophy of ministry, and it will never happen unless leaders sit down and talk through the right questions: What's true about the people we want to reach? What motivates them? What turns them off? What works? What doesn't work? Are we arranging ministry to be most effective?

But the time and energy this requires is an invaluable investment. It gives us a clear picture of our target audience and an understanding of how best to minister to them.

Establish a Strategy

Determining the philosophy of ministry often results in a long list of ideas and concepts. The next step is to synthesize them into a strategic plan and then set priorities.

On the basis of the information we'd gathered in our evangelism think tank, we defined four groups of people, two groups of unbelievers and two of believers:

Nonchurched Harrys. Nonchurched Harry doesn't attend Willow Creek or any other church. On Sunday morning he pops open a beer in anticipation of the Bears game. He has no interest in God.

Seekers. These spiritually sensitive people are looking for something, and sometimes they come to church. But they've not yet become Christians.

Average believers. The word *evangelism* scares this group to death. They know they ought to evangelize, but they have neither the will nor the training to attempt it.

Zealots. These folks have the gift of evangelism. They want to do evangelism. Their challenge is to use their gift effectively, without unnecessarily turning people off.

How can we involve all these people in evangelism? Obviously it requires four different approaches. So we formulated a goal for each group:

— To get Nonchurched Harry seeking.

— To help the seeker become a believer.

— To take the fear out of evangelism for the average believer and to make witnessing a natural part of life.

— To organize the zealots so they aren't randomly alienating people but are wisely deployed for concerted evangelism.

Then we detailed our philosophy for each group. What's true about Nonchurched Harry? What's true about seekers? And on down the list. Once we knew what each group needed, we could develop a strategy just for them.

We couldn't however, attack on all four fronts simultaneously; we had to establish priorities. So we asked this question: Where can we make the greatest impact with our initial investment? We realized our zealots were vastly outnumbered by our average believers. If we could turn loose these average masses, we'd make a major impact. So we decided the average believers would be our first target group.

Our strategy to move them into active evangelism was to remove their fears, build their confidence, and give them the needed tools. We scheduled a four-week evangelism seminar on consecutive Monday nights. We taught people how to give their testimony, answer the ten toughest questions, and present the gospel in a clear, concise way. In the last year, one fourth of our committed believers have taken the seminars.

The response has been varied. If zero is complete fear and ten is ease in sharing one's faith, some people have inched from zero to one, while others have zoomed up to ten. I know one man who had the joy of leading two people to Christ in the two months following the seminar.

Now that we have the seminars in place, we're moving on to the zealots. Our strategy is to equip them and put them into organized evangelistic groups. For example, we've started a class called Foundations that meets each week to handle the tough issues that come up when we confront our culture with the gospel.

"Does God Cause Earthquakes?" was the subject of a Foundations class two weeks after the devastating quake in San Francisco. Previously, we'd handled biblical authority, damnation, suffering, reincarnation, and others. We probably won't address issues like these in depth on Sunday mornings, but a number of our people come early on Wednesday evenings to tackle them.

We've already begun to reach seekers through our Sunday morning services designed especially for them. We feel weakest in our response to Nonchurched Harry. But we chose to focus on the other three groups first, because they are the keys to reaching Harry.

We do, however, aim one aspect of our ministry — our newspaper advertising — directly at the nonchurched. We ask ourselves, *What section of the paper do they read? And what kind of ad grabs their attention? A picture of a steeple? No. They prefer something more like a movie ad that looks interesting and addresses their needs.* So we put enticing, need-oriented ads in among the movie notices. Some visitors tell us they first came to Willow Creek because of these ads.

We're also building a sports ministry. If we can intermingle evangelist/athletes with Nonchurched Harrys in our softball or basketball leagues, build relationships, and expose outsiders to the church, we're on our way toward evangelism. When they say, *This isn't so bad. I wonder what their church service is like?*, they're on the verge of becoming a seeker.

Direct the Resources

Identifying a leader, determining a purpose, and formulating a philosophy and strategy are the tough parts of ministry. The fun part is actually making the ministry happen — allocating the finances, setting the times, and deploying the people.

Over the past fourteen years, I've spent hundreds and hundreds of hours in meetings, pounding out ministry plans. The reward comes when I see the ministry take shape and change lives.

One group we're just beginning to unleash is called Defenders. This group is made up of hard-core apologists, men and women who have a heart for the intellectual issues and tough questions of faith. They like nothing better than researching thorny issues such as the problem of pain or creation versus evolution.

Now when anyone gets stuck on a difficult question, there is someone to turn to. Our staff directs both questions and questioners to them. People witnessing to their friends have someone to help them with challenging arguments.

What a resource God has allowed us to activate — a group of Defenders dedicated to leading skeptics to Christ! It's their passion.

And it's my passion, too. That's why I'm committed to the five steps outlined above. I want to launch ministries that work, that fulfill the purposes of the church, that reach the lost and lead them toward maturity in Christ.

There are many techniques and practices that every church can employ to insure efficient and proper use of funds. In most cases they also happen to be techniques that engender trust.

— Arthur DeKruyter

CHAPTER SEVEN

Overseeing Church Finances

Knowing the right ways to raise and spend money is a key task of anyone who helps manage a church. But there's an often-overlooked prerequisite to good money management: trust. A church doesn't need money as much as it needs trust. Without trust, a church will always have money problems. By addressing the trust issue, a church has taken a major step toward financial health.

About twelve years ago, a woman was tragically killed in this community. Having no church home, the family asked if Christ Church of Oak Brook would hold the services. Without hesitation, we did. Subsequently, the widower became intrigued by the church that was willing to help his family, to offer genuine comfort in their grief. He began attending our services.

He studied us carefully. He wanted to know how our ministries functioned, how we made decisions, how we handled money. He concluded that our ministry had integrity. He then decided that he wanted to support a church that helped the community like we had helped him. He has not yet become a member of our church, but he attends, and for the last twelve years he has donated to our church nearly as much as our largest giver.

When people trust the integrity of a ministry, they willingly give to it.

On the other hand, questions about trust can dry up giving. Not long ago, a woman in another congregation told me she was going to stop giving to her church, of which she is a charter member. She would still give to the denomination's missions, but never would she give another penny to that congregation. She didn't trust those making the spending decisions. She felt the church budget had been used to underwrite the minister's pet causes, paying for his travels and donating to movements he supports. She assumed he had manipulated the budget-making process.

Obviously there are two sides to the issue, but the point is clear: when people don't trust the integrity of the leadership structure, finances will become an increasing problem.

Consequently, to address how we oversee church finances, the overarching principle is to build and maintain trust.

The Pastor's Personal Role

The integrity of a church rests with the leader. That statement isn't new, but it has proven true time and again. Just as the character of a corporation is shaped by its leader, so the pastor's integrity bleeds through the whole congregation. As people see the way we, as ministers, handle our own and the church's money, this will determine whether they trust us and whether they will gladly give to the church.

I have found I can build trust, and a financially healthy congregation, if I adhere to a few principles.

● *Don't snub church finances.* Although some people question whether a minister should be concerned with finances, I don't see how a minister can avoid them. Ideally, I'd love to be free to do nothing but preach and pray and let others tend tables. But that isn't reality. Even in the Book of Acts, the apostles found themselves involved with finances — recognizing the tensions over benevolences, restructuring lines of authority, establishing deacons. Later, the apostle Paul not only taught about money, he also solicited gifts and delivered them to needy churches — all elements of financial management.

Today, every pastor has similar financial responsibilities. We teach Christian principles about money. We help decide where to invest the church's resources in ministry, both in the congregation and abroad. We interpret for the church — through sermons and newsletters — the financial state of the church. In short, we need to be aware of the church's financial situation.

● *Use abilities wisely.* Any of us ministers, no matter our abilities and talents, can oversee church finances effectively. But first we need to recognize our strengths and weaknesses and oversee accordingly.

For example, take two recent presidents of the United States. Jimmy Carter was a veritable walking encyclopedia; he was involved in all aspects of his administration. He knew the details, but his weakness was lack of delegation. He wanted to know so much of what was going on that it limited how much could happen.

Ronald Reagan, on the other hand, delegated everything. He was a great communicator and could effectively explain, in broad strokes, the goals of the nation. But if you asked him about details of the government or policy, he often didn't have the foggiest idea. He knew to whom he entrusted responsibility, but that was all.

Likewise, some ministers like to keep their hands on financial details. Some are better at delegating. Some can articulate the big picture; others revel in monthly reports. Some love to fiddle with numbers; others just want to see the bottom line. Some can make financial judgments with ease; others struggle to make money decisions. No matter what our natural inclination, we shouldn't disqualify ourselves from the financial aspects of ministry.

The pastor who is gifted in financial matters can engender trust through demonstrating competence. The pastor who has few gifts in financial matters can build trust, too, by seeking advice and delegating work intelligently to people of character. If we recognize our limitations and seek able help when necessary, then, when we speak about money, as we often must, the congregation will know that although we are not experts, we consult some before we open our mouths.

● *Model giving (They'll find out if you don't!).* I've known some ministers who are poor givers. They never tithe, much less go beyond it. They have their reasons: They believe the giving of themselves to the church is enough. In some cases, they feel their pay is so low they can't afford to tithe.

Even if I accept their reasons, their practice has a deadening effect on their ministry. It sabotages their efforts to teach stewardship.

Some naive souls imagine they can keep their level of giving from their congregations. This is supposed to be privileged information. But people have ways of finding out. What the minister contributes is hot news. Everybody wants to know: Does the pastor tithe? Does he give to the building-fund drive? How much? When other causes come up, is he generous or tight? Sooner or later, word gets out about what kind of giver the pastor is, and that sets the tone for ministry.

I knew one minister who preached marvelous sermons on giving. He was one of the key leaders of his denomination. But within his own congregation, a nucleus of his board knew his giving, or lack of it. And they resented it. "He's a marvelous preacher," one of them once commented to me, "but he doesn't give a nickel to the church. How can he expect us to give when he doesn't?"

He had undercut his ability to develop a giving congregation. Ministers who give significantly not only create a climate of giving, but their generosity also will build trust like nothing else can.

In addition to a personal role, we pastors also do well to take a professional role in overseeing church finances. Here are some of the ways I do that.

Review the Budget at the Earliest Stages

How each church initiates the budget will differ, but at the beginning of the process, the pastor's role is crucial. Since I am one of the few involved in the overall operation of our church, I review the budget at its earliest stages.

In our church the department heads propose their budgets, and our business manager, our treasurer, and I see those proposals before they get to the full board. That way, I have a chance, for instance, to ask why the youth department wants significantly more than last year.

That doesn't mean I have dictatorial powers. The treasurer can disagree and talk with me before things go to the board. In addition, it is the full board that decides the final budget, as well as any disagreements the treasurer and I have.

Nonetheless, going over the budget ahead of time saves unnecessary wrangling at the board level. It also insures that all the departments, especially the unglamorous ones, get treated fairly in the budget process. So at this stage I usually sit down with the various departments and negotiate.

Once, for example, the education department desperately wanted some new equipment. Yet, because of our church's priorities, I asked them to hold back. The counseling department needed the funding that year. So the education people postponed their plan until we got the counseling department set up. A year later they came back and rightly asked, "Now is it our turn?"

Of course, such negotiation requires good relationships all around. But I have found if I get my department heads together and plead fairness, nobody will fight for his own skin at the expense of others. Each wants the church to rise as a whole.

The pastor who can monitor the budget at the earliest stages will limit political wrangling and encourage team play. And that will build trust naturally in the church.

Know Who Gives What Only When It's Critical

Some ministers believe they should know exactly how much various individuals give to the church. They believe the checkbook is a barometer of a person's spirituality, and knowing a person's giving pattern is necessary for proper pastoral care. Other pastors don't want to know what their people give; they feel it's a private matter between the person and the Lord.

I come down in the middle on this issue. I do not need to know what everybody gives to the church. I assume they're all good givers until I have reason to believe otherwise. So I prefer not to know.

Except in certain instances. When I am looking for a trustee or someone to chair a building-fund drive, I will examine what the candidate has contributed to the church. If I am choosing the missions committee chairperson, I investigate how he or she donates to missions. I cannot expect people to follow someone who is not a giver, and I cannot expect people to give if the leaders of a giving program do not give, themselves.

So, I will examine people's giving, but only on rare occasions. It's like a reference, a character check. And even in these situations, I'm not after specific amounts. I just want to know if the person gives more than a token amount.

Obtain a Legitimate Audit

Every church, large or small, needs to audit itself annually. It not only will protect the treasurer and keep the church out of legal trouble, it also will build trust.

The audit can be performed by someone outside the church. Or, if there is a good CPA in the church, he or she can be used. But even if a church has to spend money to do it, I think the church should get an audit. It will pay dividends in trust.

Make Money People Ministry Minded

The finance people in a church are often powerful people who, deliberately or not, subvert the intention of the congregation. They often ask not, "What do we want to do as a church?" but "Can we afford it?" After all, it's their job to ask that question. But that question often wins board discussions hands down — and that is not right. This can foster distrust among the congregation if members feel that the financial people are dictating policy despite the will of the congregation.

One way to deal with this potential problem is to integrate the finance people and the ministry people. In our case, we've put our trustees and elders together. Our trustees are part of the elder board that oversees the ministry. A majority of the elders have committee responsibilities. The trustee elders are relieved of serving on other committees because of their work as trustees, but in every other way they're treated as part of the elder board.

Trustees do not report to the elder board; trustees are elders. The whole group is involved in decisions of the board. When they go back to planning finances — which remains their prerogative — they know exactly what's in the mind of the elders. They tend, then, to be ministry minded as well as financially concerned.

Train for Right Attitudes at the Right Time

Naturally, it can be extremely hard for a board to manage money in a Christian way unless the pastor ingrains the principles of Christian stewardship within them. And that takes years of education, timely education.

For example, I don't preach on stewardship at the end of the year, or when we're having a fund-raising drive. I preach on it in the normal flow. If I teach people stewardship when the pressure isn't so great, when the time comes, they're used to practicing proper stewardship.

In addition, I work with the board far in advance to educate them about the church's stewardship of money and resources. We then set guidelines about the church accepting money and memorial gifts. Then, when someone comes with a gift or request, we simply review the adopted policy of the board.

If we've not adopted a policy on a financial matter that has come before the board, and if the board seems insistent on doing something I think is inappropriate, that is no time to get into an emotional battle. I let that decision go. But six months later, I bring up the subject and try to get a policy established.

Crisis is the wrong time to begin training. It's like the old Scotsman said: The time to put the shingles on the roof is not during the rain storm, when you need them, but in the sunshine, when you don't need them.

Assume a "We" Stance

Some boards act like they are to make spending decisions and the congregation exists to pick up the tab. In some churches, board and congregation never jointly agree about the budget, let alone the identity and purpose of the church. Naturally, that leads to tension.

There is always some "us-them" tension in a church — the "us" being the leaders who decide how to spend money and therefore need to raise it, and the "them" being the congregation who subscribe the budget. You can't get away from that completely. But we prefer to stress the "we" aspects of church life: *we* are the church; *we* own the church; *we* operate the church; *we* are blessed by the church. Whenever we present anything, whether it's in the bulletin or from the pulpit, it's always "we." It is not what *you* have to do to raise *the church's* budget. It's what *we* need to do to raise *our* budget.

Consequently, we don't try to "sell" a budget to people. We present the budget. If the people don't like something in it, that's okay. It's their prerogative to vote it down and live without that service or ministry. The budget belongs to all of us.

Adopt Policies to Prevent Problems

When policies are adopted and followed consistently, small groups or individuals cannot manipulate the system. That is the major cause of distrust between a congregation and board — that a few are dictating policy contrary to the will of the majority. Naturally, when boards cave in to special-interest seekers, the average parishioner becomes increasingly reluctant to give to the church — "Let the wealthy donors carry the whole thing." In the end, the wealthy person gets increasing power and also carries most of the financial responsibility, which is unhealthy for any institution. But consistent policies help prevent preferential treatment and help build trust.

For instance, I have had some of the largest donors in the church ask me if they could borrow some of the church's tables and chairs for a family gathering. Other people want to borrow the big pans or coffee urns from the church kitchen. Others have asked to use a church room to celebrate a twenty-fifth anniversary.

Because of the number of requests we receive, our policy is not to permit people to hold private parties here. Furthermore, we don't loan out anything — chairs, urns, microphones, nothing — other than for a church function.

But that policy is tested often. What do you do if a person who has donated more than the value of the whole kitchen wants to borrow a couple of large roasting pans? It's not easy, but I've had to say no. If you make exceptions for the privileged few, you've lost your trust in the eyes of everyone else.

The tough part is saying no the first time. Once you've made it stick, then everybody understands the policy, and they'll respect you for it.

The board, therefore, must establish and stick to its policies. I believe this principle applies to the small church, as well. Yes, the small church usually is run by relationships rather than priorities, but certain policies ought to be adhered to nonetheless. If not, we risk the long-range trust and thus the financial health of the church.

Meet Felt Needs to Pay for Unfelt Needs

Every church budget contains items that respond to both felt and unfelt needs of the congregation. Sunday school material, choral music, and salaries are expenses that make a direct impact on the congregation. If they are not paid for, the congregation immediately senses a problem. Thus, there is adequate understanding and lobbying for such needs at budget time.

But no congregation can minister in the name of Christ without also budgeting for unfelt needs: choir and youth group trips, long-term repairs, the church library. These are the type of things congregations may object to, and, if the budget seems tight or if they are angry about something else, these items can become the battle-ground that causes the entire budget to be disapproved.

I have found, however, that if we meet felt needs, people will support programs happily that do not meet felt needs.

Take the music budget, for example. No one questions the need for choir music. No one has ever objected to choir robes. Some, however, might question whether the choir should be subsidized to put on concerts outside the church. You can spend several thousand dollars on a concert that might attract only a few hundred people.

But a community concert makes an important statement to the community. And preparing for the challenge of special events improves the quality of the choir. Besides, it's good for morale, especially if you happen to have a lot of dedicated singers and musicians who like to do more than just sing hymns.

Nonetheless, some members may look at the music budget and ask why it's so high. But if we are meeting the musical needs, as well as other felt needs, of our congregation, their trust level will be higher. They know we are spending money wisely on areas that directly affect them. They then will logically assume we are spending it wisely on things that don't directly concern them. An explanation is always necessary, but there will be less tendency to question every penny when felt needs have been met.

Don't Do Fund Raising (Do Sell Bonds)

Commitment to the spiritual program must remain central if a congregation is to continue to give to the church. Because fund raisers tend to place the emphasis on the money raised rather than the ministry supported, we don't have them. Our policy is that our church ministries will be paid for by the budget. If we sense people don't want to support it in the budget, we cut it out. We do not turn around and sponsor large fund-raising programs in order to fund special projects or make up deficits.

Granted, pastors sometimes find themselves in churches where, as part of the tradition, there are strawberry sundae sales, or bake sales, or bazaars, or rummage sales. I confess I encouraged such in my first church, much to my regret.

I thought up countless schemes. I had a brother-in-law in the wholesale produce business, and I bought Michigan strawberries by the carload. We had practically everybody in town buy strawberries from us, and we made money. We organized steak fries, car washes, bake sales, and even hat sales.

But people began resenting this. They would be confronted at Bible studies and youth groups by people selling tickets or produce. The members, of course, often would buy out of a sense of loyalty. But they didn't need these things. So their resentment built because they felt obligated to buy something they didn't want in order to support the church.

So, if a church has a tradition of fund raisers, it would be best to wean the congregation from them, slowly grafting those causes onto the church budget. And if people won't put them into the church budget, well, a church may want to evaluate if those are significant ministries.

Let me make a distinction here, however. I do endorse the idea of churches selling bonds to their people to raise money. That's entirely different. People aren't *donating* a nickel; buying a bond is an interest-earning *investment* in something spiritually worthwhile. Rather than a bank using the money, a church does. Since buying bonds has nothing whatsoever to do with tithing and giving to the church, members are still expected to give. But money they plan to invest anyway might as well be invested in the church.

Misappropriation of Funds

Finally, we come to the sticky issue of misappropriation of funds, the one thing that can unnerve a congregation the most and undercut years of trust. How do we deal with it to minimize the damage?

What do you do if, for example, you suspect someone is misusing church funds? What if someone may be keeping part of the offering or shifting funds from a church account to a personal account? In the rare instances when this has happened to us, this is our approach:

First, with the board's approval, I have the church books audited. If an annual audit has already been performed but has failed to check the suspected problem, we will create a system that will check it. If we think a staff member is using petty cash for personal expenses, for example, we might begin insisting that receipts be kept for even small purchases.

In such a case, I go to the suspected person and remind him of the trust he holds in handling the church's money. I suggest such a position requires there be not the least suggestion that funds are being mismanaged. To affirm publicly his integrity and that of the church, I tell him we will be starting this new policy. All along I ask him if he too doesn't think this a good procedure to protect everyone concerned.

When I have had to do this, the person usually goes along with me up to this point. But some will balk when I suggest specific procedures and dates to get the system working. However, I find if I work through the principles first, they are less likely to become defensive. If they do get defensive or evasive, this opens the way to a frank discussion of the alleged problems. Even then, to begin with principles directs their anger away from me. I'm not confronting them; the principles are.

Let's say, however, that through the special or regular audit we discover, in fact, that money has been mishandled. In that case, I call a board member in whom I have great confidence. I explain what I have discovered, and together we make an appointment with the guilty party.

When we all get together, I say to the guilty party, "Our last audit showed some problems. For example, can you explain this?" By this time the person is feeling the pressure. When it's obvious to everyone that the person is guilty, I'll approach him pastorally and say, "I don't know why you did this. Maybe you're having a problem, and you thought this was the way out. Want to tell us about it?" As pastor, one of my jobs is to point the person toward help.

At the same time, I am still the church's administrator. So I have to be firm and tell him what he already knows: that he no longer can hold his job. I ask the person for the church books and freeze any appropriate accounts. We also discuss with the person how he is going to behave in the future and whether or not restitution will be made. If the person is repentant, he will seek ways to compensate the church. If not, often there's nothing we can do but let him go. It is our policy not to prosecute in such a case. That seems to us to be the clear teaching of the Bible. We don't take a brother to court, because we are to handle these things in the household of God.

So, I respond to misappropriation both as the person's pastor and the church's administrator. I try to redeem the person and care for the institution.

Some may wonder if that combination is possible, or if two different people should perform these two different functions. I say it's vital that I do both. It's a situation in which I can model Christ's love — a love that cares enough to hold people accountable and that shows concern for another's situation. Furthermore, I demonstrate what I've been preaching for years: how such love is to be practiced in the marketplace.

One of the best things I can do for the repentant person is to call him some time later and ask him to do something for me. I, as the one who has confronted him, can show him that I also forgive him and want to start over with him. When I've done that, it's amazing the way people come back to life. When I terminate people, they naturally think I am angry with them. When I offer them a responsibility later, they discover I'm not, and they can hardly believe it. It helps them see the power of the gospel at work. And some of these people have returned to work with me in special capacities.

You can see that from beginning to end I am concerned about trust. Yes, there are many techniques and practices that every church can employ to insure efficient and proper use of funds. But in most cases they also happen to be techniques that engender trust. And that is why they encourage good stewardship and nurture a financially healthy church.

Church facilities have the potential to distract, or to communicate an unwanted message. At their best, they can glorify God and invite people into Christian fellowship.
— *Leith Anderson*

CHAPTER EIGHT

Overseeing the Building and Grounds

Whenever I attend another church, I notice what the surroundings communicate. If the bulletin says, "Hymn — to be announced," or if the sermon title is missing, it suggests that worship may not have been properly prepared. Likewise with the building and grounds: if the exterior doors look weathered, or the parking lot stripes have faded to invisibility, I wonder how much people care about their church.

Little things say a lot. And the seemingly minor elements of our building and grounds also say a lot, particularly to newcomers.

For example, during the week groups that use the sanctuary some-times move the American flag and don't think about how it's put back. But during worship a visitor may be bemused that the eagle atop the staff is facing backwards.

That illustration may seem silly, but the point is that church facilities have the potential to distract, or to communicate an un-wanted message. At their best, they can glorify God and invite people into Christian fellowship.

The Pastor's Role

As pastor, I have been involved in minor building-and-grounds decisions, for example, the placement of mirrors in the hallway and the size of brick for the building. Some people wonder why I fiddle with such details. In essence, they're asking, "What is the pastor's role in the building and grounds? Should pastors stick to leading worship and preaching, or should they also help decide the color of paint in the nursery?"

The answer varies in each situation, but several guidelines have helped me establish the level of pastoral involvement in build-ing and grounds.

1. Delegate responsibility but demonstrate interest. During a ma-jor building project, I may spend no more than half an hour a week on it. The building committee includes people who understand building issues far better than I. They give me information, and I attend meetings of the building committee (or a subcommittee), but for the most part, other people choose the pews and pick the colors. Unless a decision involves something critical or affects me personally, I delegate.

My role is not to make all the decisions, but to support those who are responsible for them. The public statements a pastor makes about a building project establish the congregation's attitude to-ward it, so I craft what I say. I explain how the building furthers the corporate mission, I thank those directly involved, and I demon-strate that I know and care about the project.

2. Concentrate energies on areas that relate to pastoral duties. The stress levels of concrete in a proposed church building don't directly affect pastoral ministry (unless there's an earthquake). But other aspects of the building do affect ministry, and during decisions about these, a pastor needs to communicate specific preferences.

Pastors usually counsel people in their offices, and the office surroundings affect that interaction. When the building committee planned Wooddale's current building, I asked that the proposed pastor's office have a parlor separate from the study area. In this parlor, there are no fluorescent lights, only table lamps. It is the only room in the building that has a pad under the carpet, and it is furnished with warm, comfortable furniture such as might be found in a family room. These simple, relatively inexpensive modifications help to achieve an important pastoral purpose: to help people relax and talk openly.

Decisions on sanctuary furnishings also call for pastoral involvement. During plans for Wooddale's new sanctuary, I asked for several specific qualities in the baptistery to make the baptism experience more relaxed and meaningful to those involved. The water will be heated, so that people don't get chilled. The baptistery includes an area in which people can get acclimated to the water before coming into public view. The top of the front of the baptistery is glass so that the congregation can see the water; this makes the ordinance more meaningful to them. Since I am right-handed, the baptistery is designed primarily for a right-handed person; this allows me to concentrate on ministry rather than the mechanics.

Sometimes a staff person will say to me, "The way the building committee designed this room, it will not work for my program." Again, because this part of the building affects pastoral duties, it is my responsibility to represent the staff and try to get that corrected.

3. Become knowledgeable in the areas of pressing concern. I'm not an expert on Arianism, but if I were preaching a sermon series on the four great heresies, I'd work at becoming one. The week of the message on Arianism, I would read theology and church history — enough so that when I stepped to the pulpit, I would be knowledgeable.

Similarly, pastors don't need to know a lot about church buildings and grounds — until it's time to decide something critical. I never knew much about acoustics until the church began planning a new sanctuary. If preaching was going to be heard by anyone in the new building, the sound system needed to be constructed properly. In order to enter those discussions, I studied about reverberation times and decibel levels. Pastors don't need to be knowledgeable about every area of the building and grounds. But they need to become conversant in the subjects currently under discussion.

4. Teach people to notice what facilities communicate. When the new pastor of one Baptist church arrived, he told the trustees, "We need to do something about the grass in the parking lot."

"We don't have any grass in the parking lot," they said.

"Come outside," he told them. Once there, they noticed the grass growing through cracks. They had driven over that grass for ten years and hadn't seen it — until they looked at it as a newcomer would.

Each year, I take the staff through the building. In each room, I ask, "If you were a first-time visitor, what would you notice?"

The answers range from "Last week's bulletin sitting on top of the piano" to "Sunday school papers left behind." Members of a church don't normally pay attention to these things, but walking through the building like this sensitizes them to the effect a building can have.

I regularly tell people that if they see a piece of paper on the ground, they should pick it up; if something isn't working, they should tell the custodian it needs to be fixed. In short, as pastor I emphasize that the building is everyone's responsibility.

The Building's Purpose

Church facilities should be consistent with the purpose of the church. Since Wooddale's purpose involves "bringing lives into harmony with God," our building should help people want to come here to worship God, and once here, to feel at home.

The expectations for church facilities vary, of course, with the community. A building in Harlem, New York, should be different from one in Haarlem, Holland. Yet, for most congregations from middle-class America, the expectations will be much the same.

Several years ago Wooddale conducted a survey and found that in suburban Minneapolis, *church* is a positive word. People here are accustomed to buildings that look and feel like churches, so the planning committee decided that the new sanctuary would have a traditional, Gothic appearance.

Near Wooddale, a church meets in a warehouse. At first, the informal setting helped in reaching less-traditional people. But after ten years, it has helped stall growth, because it runs counter to prevailing community expectations.

A corollary of the expectations principle: Most people become slightly disoriented, often subconsciously, if an individual room doesn't conform to its purpose — for example, if the sanctuary looks like a gymnasium, or a classroom looks like a library. Instead, the worship center ought to look like a worship center, classrooms like classrooms, offices like offices, and nursery like a nursery.

Wooddale never used to have symbols, not even a cross, in the worship center. When people objected, I explained, "We don't have a cross because we worship a risen Christ." True, but I overlooked the fact that visitors, who may have been unchurched for thirty years, grew up worshiping in buildings in which there was a cross. In suburban Minneapolis, at least, a cross is part of cultural expectations for a sanctuary. So we enlisted a craftsman to build a wooden cross.

An Evangelistic Building

Wooddale wants to be a church that reaches out to people. One strategy for doing that is to make our building available to the community. We have invited businesses to hold events here. Rusty Scupper, a restaurant chain, held its annual staff party in our building. Outsiders use our gym. The bloodmobile comes here. We hope the building will someday be used as a voting precinct. In short, the facility is regularly and consistently used by and for the community.

Why? Because the hardest time to get someone into the building is the first time. If people come for a community event and learn how to get here and where to park, they will feel more comfortable in visiting on Sunday.

(We have, however, established limits on the building's use. It is not used for weddings of non-Wooddale members. That may seem inconsistent, but in our theology of marriage, weddings aren't an outreach activity. In addition, we don't allow alcoholic beverages to be served in the building.)

A Reason for Every Decision

I won't argue about the color of the nursery. But I will argue that a church should have a reason for the color it chooses. It's not enough to say, "I like this color, and I don't like that one." Instead, churches need to ask, "What is this going to mean in twenty years? What does this communicate to the visitor? What is the meaning behind this?"

Here are several areas in which conscious decisions can aid a church in fulfilling its mission.

Colors. The Christian Science Church near Denver Seminary is white. In fact, many Christian Science buildings are white or off-white. It's not a coincidence that Christian Science practioners don't believe in sin or death.

In one Pentecostal church in Ohio, the back of each seat is black, but the front is red. The idea: go in reminded of your sin, and come out recognizing the blood of Christ.

In short, color has meaning; it makes emotional impressions and has theological implications that need to be considered.

For example, building committees often are dominated by men, and men tend to choose blue. But blue gives a "cold" feeling, not a feeling of warmth and intimacy, to many people in our culture. Green, for some reason, is not a positive color in our society. Almost never will a business executive wear a green suit, and few best-sellers use green on their cover. When green is used in natural landscaping, it is accepted, but it rarely will succeed as a central interior color.

Further, colors have lifespans. Orange was popular in the

sixties, black and pink in the fifties. Many homes built in the late fifties or early sixties have bathrooms tiled in black and pink. Mauve is widely used in the late 1980s. Mauve was suggested as the integrating color scheme in Wooddale's new building, but the idea was later discarded because mauve probably will pass away in popularity.

Which colors last? In the cathedrals, and in churches and homes that have stood for hundreds of years, the predominant colors usually are white, brown, and red.

Women's service areas. Usually, women decide which church a family will attend. The most important areas, therefore, in making a church building attractive to visitors, are the woman's restroom and the nursery, for women will most likely use and notice these.

The ladies' room, then, needs to be clean, spacious, accessible, well marked, and brightly lit. We have placed mirrors in hallways outside the restroom so that women who only want to check their hair don't congest the rest room. (Also, because more and more fathers are changing diapers, in our new facility the men's rooms will have diaper-changing tables as well.)

It's vital that the nursery be attractive. Baby boomers have fewer children, and they spend a lot of money and attention on them. They expect high-quality children's facilities.

Hallways. One mistake in the design of our current building was that the ceilings are too low and the hallways too narrow. Between services, hallways were congested, and people felt cramped. When we raised the ceiling and widened hallways, it not only eased traffic, but it also encouraged fellowship, which often takes place in hallways. The higher ceiling gives the hallways a less-confining feel, and the wider hallways permit tables for coffee and refreshments.

Sanctuary. Consultants say that facial expressions can be seen from a distance no greater than eighty-five feet. So our proposed sanctuary places all seats within that distance. It also eliminates pillars, which interfere with sound and sight. Because in our community most people expect pews, it will use those rather than individual seats.

Acoustics. Sometimes people come away from a church service irritated, but they don't know why. In some cases, the reason is poor acoustics, particularly if people *see* the speaker in one place and *hear* the voice through speakers elsewhere. In most televisions, for example, the sound comes from near the picture. Occasionally I'll visit a home in which the television is wired to the stereo system, and the sound comes from an area far from the picture. Most people cannot tolerate that for long. As a result, many churches are now clustering speakers toward the front center of the sanctuary.

The key acoustical challenge for churches is to provide an environment that serves both music and preaching. Music calls for a long reverberation time; speaking requires a short one. In the Basilica of St. Mary, the reverberation time is seven seconds: a person can utter a sound and still hear it seven seconds later. This may be wonderful for some choral singing, but it makes human speech almost unintelligible. For Wooddale's new sanctuary, we settled on a reverberation time just under three seconds. That's rather long for speaking but long enough to satisfy musicians.

Safety. To make people feel comfortable, it's important to insure their safety. We asked local fire and police departments to analyze our building and recommend safety improvements. We now hold fire drills twice a year. An emergency procedure sheet is stored in the pulpit; if an alarm sounds, the person in front reads it to instruct people how to vacate the building. We also developed a procedure for getting babies out of the nursery in an emergency.

Employing Expertise

Because there are so many concerns in designing an effective building, for major projects, it is vital to use knowledgeable consultants. They bring trained, outsiders' eyes; they see things we cannot.

I unintentionally functioned as a consultant while on vacation one Sunday after Christmas. I attended a pastor friend's church. My family and I were late as we drove into the parking lot — typical of visitors, because they have trouble finding the church and don't know where to park. We were directed to park at what seemed to be the other end of the world. As we walked back to the buildings in subzero temperatures, we noticed several empty parking places labeled, Reserved for Staff. By the time I walked into the service, I was not a happy man.

Later my friend called and asked me about my impressions. I told him, "From a visitor's point of view, it looks like you care more about your absentee staff than about visitors. You save parking places for staff members who don't come and make your visitor walk huge distances in subzero weather to get to church." He hadn't realized the problem, because he and his staff have dozens of things to think about on Sunday morning, and they hadn't considered the effect of their parking on the newcomer. It took an outside "consultant" to point it out, but then they immediately improved the situation.

At Wooddale, we have hired an acoustician, a landscape architect, and even an educator to help us design the nursery. In the long run, consultants lead to a better facility and savings in not having to redo expensive projects. Even small churches can tap skilled community people who will offer counsel for very little or even free. If I were in rural Minnesota in a region with several smaller churches, I would try to set up a consortium. Six churches could each contribute one person to an evaluation team; over three years the team would visit each church and evaluate it.

Another type of "free consulting" is to visit other churches. Our building committee has spent many evenings visiting other churches in our area. The committee members have seen other sanctuaries and listened to other sound systems. This adds to their knowledge when planning.

Front-End Investments

Finally, pastors need to deal with two key concerns that people have about buildings.

The first is that new buildings (and remodeling old ones) cost big money. Whenever such expenditures are contemplated, the pastor will be asked, "Couldn't that money be better used for missions or to feed the poor?"

That tension is inevitable, and every church has to decide how to balance concern for facilities and concern for mission. In our case, we have decided to spend money on the building because we see it as an investment for mission.

When Wooddale relocated several years ago, we spent a lot of money. But we dramatically increased the number of people that we reach. That enlarged our missions giving and the number of people going into missionary service. Although we put a lot of money into buildings, it was like a high front-end investment. Once that investment has been made, the building lasts for a long time, and meanwhile, we have a larger base of operation for missions. The initial cost is disproportionate but for a limited time.

Consider a young couple buying their first home. At first, they have to commit an uncomfortable percentage of their income to the mortgage payment. Later, as inflation takes its course and they advance in their careers, the payments become manageable. But all along the house is theirs to use for greater ends, like raising children.

Ministry versus Maintenance

A second question that buildings raise, and pastors need to answer, is: How much should the building be used? The question pits ministry against maintenance.

While I was serving a previous church, the congregation hired as custodian a man recently retired from a successful banking career. Being a precise person, he wanted to get and keep the building in perfect shape. A few weeks into his tenure, after he had made the building immaculate, some kids playing baseball on the church's front lawn hit a baseball through a window of the sanctuary. The broken glass littered the pews. Our custodian was furious; he refused to return the kids' baseball until they fixed the window. The kids got their parents, and everybody ended up on the church lawn, neighbors and custodian confronting one another. The parents ended up calling me at home, and I had to come and intercede. Eventually, I managed to get the ball and give it back to the kids, but the custodian didn't approve.

The church's goal was to introduce these people to Jesus

Christ. The custodian's goal was to clean up the glass, get a new window, and teach these kids a lesson. The incident has served ever since as a reminder of the friction that can occur between those responsible for the building and those responsible for the mission of the church.

We try to ease that natural friction in three ways. First, we explain to the maintenance staff that the building is not a museum; it is meant for ministry. The building is going to have some wear and tear. Their job is to do their best at keeping it up, but the church has a higher purpose than upkeep.

Second, we honor many of our custodian's concerns. We put in stain-resistant carpeting. We do not allow any red beverage — punch, Kool-Aid, or soft drinks — in the building, because red and orange dyes cause stains.

Third, we incorporate our custodian in the larger ministry. He attends coffee breaks and prayer times with the rest of the staff. That way the pastoral staff feels more responsible for the building, and he feels more responsible for the ministry.

This kind of partnership is our goal in managing the buildings and grounds.

PART THREE
The People

Many church leaders bear incredible loads because they haven't mastered the art of raising up fellow leaders and releasing responsibility to them.

— Don Cousins

CHAPTER NINE
Working through Leaders

Growth inevitably leads to chaos. I don't mean the kind of chaos caused by weak administration or poor planning. I mean the turmoil that accompanies action, the disruption that results from change, and the problems that surface from incorporating new workers into a ministry. An organization without this kind of chaos probably isn't making much of a mark. I'll take chaos — with impact — any time over a calm lack of fruitfulness.

While chaos may not be a comfortable state, the inconveniences it brings are a small price to pay for the thrill of knowing one's ministry is making a difference. And when great things are happening in a ministry, people tend to step forward and ask, "How can I help?" They *want* to be part of the activity — even somewhat chaotic activity — when they see the fruit it bears.

The man who runs our small-group ministry owned a real estate company before he joined our staff. A year or so before he came on staff, he said to me, "I can tell my passion is changing. I used to want to pour all my time into the marketplace. Now I've tasted what it is to be used by God, and I want to invest myself more fully in things that really matter."

People like this, who arise from congregations as volunteers or paid staff, can help bear the load active ministry creates. They can be channels through which we accomplish the work of the ministry. The only catch is that they have to be properly managed.

Overcoming the Drawbacks

The pastor overloaded with demands may cringe at the prospect of recruiting and supervising other workers. If he has insufficient time to do immediate tasks, how will he ever find time to enlist others in ministry?

Unfortunately, some leaders believe their primary responsibility is to keep the ministry running smoothly, to check chaos at any cost. So they devote the bulk of their time to the immediate tasks that keep their ministry under control. They maintain the ministry. They put out fires. But they never take the steps that would move their ministry forward.

That maintenance mindset has to be reversed. Short-term focus must make way for long-term perspective. We need to ask, *What decisions or activities will help me be more effective a year from now than I am today?* The answer to that question will determine what we should do first.

Once again, it's a question of A and B priorities. B priorities maintain the ministry, and chances are, they scream the loudest for our attention. But A priorities move our ministries forward. So we need to spend the best hours of our day on A priorities, even if that means setting aside a beckoning pile of B priorities.

After fifteen years in ministry, I have concluded that recruiting and training leaders always should be near the top of a manager's A priorities. If we want our ministries to grow, we must nurture people who can take over a portion of our work and expand it. The time required to do this often seems like a drawback, but it gives us back the time in the end.

Take hospital visitation, for example. On any given day, it would be easier for a pastor to make a quick hospital visit than to recruit volunteers, take them with him, and teach them to make hospital calls. If he went by himself, he could gain time — that day. But the following year he'd still be in the same position: personally making all the hospital calls. And each call would take him away from other necessary activities.

But let's say that early in the year he invested A-priority time in recruiting and training people gifted and called by God to be hospital callers — people with potential to do it more effectively than he. By year's end, they could cover the ministry of hospital visitation and free him to pursue other A priorities. His initial investment of time would quickly save him hours each week and also enable others to use their gifts in meaningful ministry.

Many church leaders bear incredible loads because they haven't mastered the art of raising up fellow leaders and releasing responsibility to them. So they work sixty to seventy hours a week, or more, and produce less fruit than a leader who works reasonable hours but has learned to tap the potential of others.

At Willow Creek, we want our staff to be around for the long haul. We also want them and their families to enjoy life and each other; we don't want to provoke spouses to anger or cause children to grow up resenting the church for taking Mom or Dad away. So we encourage staff to limit their ministry responsibilities to an average of fifty hours a week, which includes their participation in church services and small groups.

We also know a staff member won't draw others into the kingdom or into leadership unless he exhibits joy, and joy springs from a refreshed life. Who would want to take on the mantle of ministry responsibility if it looks like one big pain?

What keeps ministry from becoming an overwhelming burden? A healthy, shared leadership role. I asked one of our singles ministry directors who came to us from a plush position in business, "Do you ever miss the marketplace? You had more freedom and less pressure, and you certainly made more money."

"No way!" he replied. "I wouldn't go back for a minute. Sure, the ministry is demanding. But I have a great team of workers who help meet the demands. With the fruit my family and I are harvesting and the sense of God's pleasure in what we're doing, there's no way I'd go back now."

Would he feel the same if he hadn't shared his ministry with others? Not on your life. The hours would be killing him, and he'd want out. Fortunately, he took the time early in his ministry to train helpers, and now he's reaping the reward of a manageable ministry. As he learned, the seeming drawback of too little time to train others is actually more of a mental block than a true drawback.

Of course, not all drawbacks are mental blocks. For example, sometimes I make mistakes in choosing people to become leaders. I invest myself in people who don't pan out or never reach the levels I expected. That's frustrating, but a reality.

Any leader must be willing to make mistakes, because we all will. One year I had to let go three staff members who were close friends of mine. All three were men of character who loved the Lord and fit our staff relationally, but their ministries had passed them by. They had ministered effectively to 150 people, but they couldn't handle 200 or 250. Their ministries were suffering, and they were under tremendous pressure.

Decisions like that are tough to make and even harder to carry out. But if we seek and obey God's direction, we can trust him to bring about a resolution in time. For a while my relationships with these former staff members were strained, because my decisions had complicated their lives. Today, however, they all are pleased with their career or ministry opportunities, and together we can thank God for his wise guidance.

Most leaders begin ministry fully intending to work through others to demonstrate the priesthood of all believers. But some have drifted away from that principle after getting burned. They selected a wrong person, and the choice came back to haunt them. If that happens three or four times early in one's ministry, the natural tendency is to decide never again to touch the hot stove.

That's unfortunate, because occasional failures don't mean the principle is defective; the practice just needs refining. When fear arises, it's time to look back and determine where the breakdown occurred: *Did my selection process fall short? Did I fail to train people properly?*

It helps to remember that Jesus was deserted by all twelve of his disciples in his hour of greatest need. If Jesus experienced that kind of fallout, who am I to think I can avoid it totally? I shouldn't quit pursuing sound practices just because of occasionally poor performance.

Other drawbacks of working through others center on the personality of the leader. Personal insecurity may make one think, *If I raise up others to do part of my work, will I lose my uniqueness, my status? And what if they use their new abilities to undercut me?* Those with an unhealthy need to be in control will hesitate to let others into the circle of responsibility.

Good leaders, on the other hand, keep their eyes on the big picture and say, "Building the kingdom of God and seeing this person develop his or her potential — even if it's greater than mine — is more important than protecting my territory."

In reality, accomplishing the work of the ministry through others usually makes the leader look better than ever. More work gets done. More ministry takes place. And the leader becomes respected as a recruiter, trainer, and delegator.

I use a circle to represent what a person can accomplish, given his or her capacities, gifts, energy, and availability. Obviously, any one person's circle is limited; it cannot expand without the addition of another person's resources. Thus, the scope of a ministry remains limited when only one person works in it.

We try to teach our staff to invest their lives in people who have the potential to do one of two things: *expand* the staff member's circle of ministry, or *replace* him or her in the circle. After two or three years of training, the one being trained ought to contribute enough to free the staff member to expand the ministry or to hand it over and move on to a new endeavor.

That has been my experience at Willow Creek. I started the high school ministry, founded our singles ministry, and then developed our small-group ministry. At each juncture, I stepped out of one responsibility and into another, primarily because someone was ready to assume my place. By grooming others to take over my responsibilities, I've freed myself to broaden the scope of our church's ministry. Had I not done so, my contribution never would have expanded beyond my initial circle of ministry in the high school department.

A leader, by implication, is a person who draws others into effective ministry. The key to doing this is to select potential associates with care.

What to Look For in Leaders

In seeking leaders, the temptation is to look first for an individual with tremendous gifts and abilities. At Willow Creek, however, we've learned that's not the place to start.

● *Character.* The number-one leadership criterion is strength of character. This cannot be compromised. Spiritual intensity or raw ability may appear more important, but we've learned the hard way that they're not.

By his mid twenties, a person's character is relatively set. If someone is hard working, honest, conscientious, and loyal in his twenties, he'll probably still be that way in his forties or sixties. Likewise, if there's a major flaw, it probably won't change without extensive work more akin to reparenting than discipleship.

A 25-year-old who doesn't tell the truth likely has worked on the art of deception since childhood; it's doubtful he'll change after one conversation about dishonesty. It's the same with a lack of personal organization or discipline. Any change would require major reweaving of the fabric of the person's character.

We've learned we can't compromise character. No matter how gifted, trained, or spiritually mature a person is, the true usefulness of those attributes will be determined by character.

How does one assess character? The two indicators I watch are how people manage their personal life and how they relate to others.

A prerequisite to leading others is the ability to lead one's own life effectively. That's what Paul meant in 1 Corinthians 9:27: "I beat my body and make it my slave so that after I have preached to others, I myself will not be disqualified for the prize" (NIV). A leader's first responsibility is to have his or her life in order. An individual who cannot exert authority over his own life won't be able to exercise healthy authority over the lives of others.

Weak character will manifest itself in a lack of self-management: poor self-discipline, tardiness with appointments, incomplete work, being controlled by outside circumstances, or even moral lapses.

Years ago we hired a staff member whose gifts and spiritual intensity appeared unquestionable. We learned after hiring him, however, that he tended to twist the truth. On numerous occasions staff members discovered he had told them conflicting stories. He eventually began pitting one staff person against another, and relationships began to break down.

He also exaggerated. We'd ask, "How many were at that meeting last night?"

"Oh, hundreds," he'd say.

When we knew differently, we'd confront him: "Was it really hundreds?"

"Well, maybe 150." Even after several conversations like this, he continued to exaggerate, and we realized his repeated exaggerations were another form of deception. We all make mistakes, but a continuing pattern such as his indicates a character flaw. Because he failed to recognize it and do anything about it, we had to let him go.

Often manifestations of character weakness aren't readily apparent. That's why it's so important to observe prospective leaders over time.

The second indicator of character is interpersonal skills. Some people can relate only in a hierarchy: up and down a chain of authority. They can work *for* people or *over* people, but they can't work *with* people. If the essence of leadership is to get close enough to people to equip them for ministry, then a key ingredient for success is the ability to work *with* people.

Interpersonal skills involve humility, courtesy, patience, self-control. Someone who exhibits these qualities likely has a healthy character and is eligible for leadership responsibility. Conversely, if a person can't relate warmly to others, I question his or her readiness to lead. I don't have time to build basic interpersonal skills into those I'm training for leadership.

Self-esteem, while not strictly a matter of character, comes sharply into play at this point. To a degree, all of us have a fragile self-esteem; all of us, because of sin, remain somewhat insecure. While that kind of universal insecurity need not hinder ministry, more pronounced insecurity definitely has a destructive effect. As I mentioned earlier, an insecure person is unable to rally strong people for fear one of them may be stronger and thus a threat.

When we interview potential staff and key lay leaders, we try to determine how they perceive themselves. Can they say, "Yes, I'm a sinner. I'm thoroughly aware that apart from the grace of God I'm nothing. But with the grace of God and the gifts he's given me, I have something to offer"? The healthier the self-esteem, the better the foundation upon which to build ministry. We've found that if we compromise here, we pay in the end.

• *Spiritual authenticity.* The second criterion for potential leaders is spiritual authenticity. Have they made a mature, consistent commitment to Christ? Does the Word of God impact their daily lives? Do they pray? Are they submitted to the Holy Spirit?

I ask specific questions to detect this quality, such as: "What have you studied in your quiet times this week? Can you share some recent answers to prayer? What are the temptations you struggle with most? How did you come to know Christ? Have you been discipled? Have you discipled someone else?" These questions get at the heart of a person's walk with God more than a general, "How's your spiritual life?"

Why must we discuss such basic spiritual issues? Because

people who carry the weight of leadership need to practice the fundamentals. A football player who says, "I don't need to practice all week. I can just go out on Sunday and play the game," is headed for trouble. Eventually his lack of preparation will catch up with him. It's the same with Christian leaders. They can't effectively promote the *product* of spirituality unless they're involved in the daily *practice* of spirituality.

● *Ministry fit.* Often people speak of ministry fit strictly in terms of gifts and abilities, but these aspects are only part of the match. Equally important is *passion*. People can be perfectly gifted for a particular ministry, but if they don't have a corresponding passion for it, they'll lose motivation and eventually quit.

We look for potential leaders who say, "God has given me a burden to work with high school students, and I've just got to figure out a way to do it." Sometimes that passion isn't evident initially, and we have to draw it out. But even then, we need to see a natural spark.

Passion is an unquenchable desire to *do* something for God. It may not manifest itself in intense emotion, but it always manifests itself in action. The passion may be as dramatic as William Booth's desire to minister to the poor, or as unassuming as a treasurer's desire to protect a church's financial integrity. In either case, God has so created and motivated a person that he or she says, "I feel strongly about this, and I have what it takes to meet the need. Let me at it!"

At Willow Creek, we have people who get emotionally charged about doing building maintenance. They want to present the unchurched a clean, inviting building on Sunday morning. They also believe the condition of our building should reflect our commitment to an excellent, perfect God. So they're excited about what they do. That's ministry fit.

● *Relational fit.* Leaders who want a well-functioning team also need to choose members who fit relationally. Christian leaders sometimes skip this point because it smacks of favoritism. Aren't we supposed to love everybody? Aren't we called to be tolerant? How, then, can we say a potential colleague might not fit relationally? For the furtherance of the kingdom, shouldn't the leader be willing to swallow his own preferences?

Yes and no. Does a leader need to be flexible? Yes. Should the leader bend to the point of selecting colleagues he or she doesn't enjoy being with? I think not. Work usually suffers when there's an uncomfortable team relationship.

Certainly we're to love everybody, but that doesn't mean we have to work closely with everybody. Why did I marry my wife instead of some other girl? One reason was that our chemistry was right. During the course of dating, I realized I liked her more than the others; we got along better; our lives meshed.

Why do I work better with some staff members? Because we happen to "click." Even if we didn't work together, we'd enjoy spending time together. Why not enhance my enthusiasm and productivity by bringing on people with whom I fit relationally?

Every work team has a unique personality. One aspect of Willow Creek's staff personality, for example, is a willingness to flex for the sake of the ministry, to share ideas, and to learn from others. Therefore, if a superstar arrives saying, "I know what I'm doing. I can handle things — my way!" he or she is going to bump heads with other staff members here. But a worker who is teachable —whether a rookie with raw abilities or an experienced veteran — will enjoy a natural relational fit.

Traits to Reconsider

While certain personality traits mark leadership candidates as obvious front runners, other traits may surprise us. In particular, we need to look carefully at aggressiveness and initiative.

Some people equate leadership with personal aggressiveness, but in reality, leaders come with a variety of styles and temperaments. Some may be quiet and lead primarily through their actions. For example, Chicago Bears linebacker and captain, Mike Singletary, doesn't say a lot, but his character and discipline make him a respected leader both on and off the field.

Other effective leaders are naturally shy and avoid the spotlight at all costs. The men who head our sound and lighting ministry don't enjoy getting up in front of people and aren't particularly social, but that doesn't hinder their ministry. They relate well to workers who also enjoy behind-the-scenes work. Their more introverted personalities are precisely what make them effective production leaders.

The key to yet other leaders' effectiveness is their sincerity. They're not aggressive; they don't push hard. But their depth of feeling and passion grip the people they lead.

Pure aggressiveness, rather than suiting a person for leadership, actually signals caution. Often, an extreme degree of aggressiveness indicates a character problem. The aggressiveness may flow from repressed anger or an inordinate desire to be successful. Such aggressiveness doesn't fuel ministry; it blows it up.

What fuels ministry is initiative. An initiator takes action, but unlike the purely aggressive person, he does it for others' sake rather than his own.

To distinguish between aggressiveness and initiative, I look at the fruit of the person's efforts. If the fruit is self-promotion, then ambitious aggression is probably at play. But if people genuinely are being helped and the ministry is growing, then initiative is more likely the spark.

In our church, I've met many businessmen who've achieved success by being shrewd and aggressive and working harder than anyone else. On the surface, they would seem to be good leadership candidates. But unless cunning individuals are submitted to the Holy Spirit and accountable to other leaders, they're like loose cannons on deck.

We place people like these under other strong leaders who can temper them. We've found that in time, the Holy Spirit can get hold of them and harness their self-will. The change usually appears first in how they treat their families or subordinates at work. Once the Holy Spirit directs their drive, they often show the makings of effective, godly leaders.

Leaders are judged, in part, by their selection of co-workers. Select the right people, and ministries thrive. Select the wrong people, and doors are opened to problems that stifle ministry and hurt credibility.

What are the keys to wise selection? Time, prayer, and discernment. Jesus didn't choose the twelve by walking along the seashore saying, "I want you and you and you. Drop your nets and follow me." In his first year of ministry, Jesus worked with a large number of disciples. When it was time to center in on potential leaders, he went away for a night of prayer, returned, and then selected the twelve (Luke 6 and Mark 3).

If Jesus needed to wait a year and pray all night, shouldn't we wait to see the fruit of potential leaders' lives? Shouldn't we pray diligently for discernment? We kid ourselves if we think we can select wisely without going through the same careful process Jesus employed.

How to Work through Others

After placing the right people in the right slots, we have to make critical decisions about which tasks to do ourselves and which to accomplish through them. Naturally, there are certain tasks we never delegate. Peter Drucker refers to those as a leader's "unique contribution," what he alone brings to the organization. Leaders shouldn't delegate what they are best positioned and gifted to accomplish.

A senior pastor, for instance, typically is gifted and trained as a teacher. Often his most significant contribution is teaching on Sunday mornings. So when he gets overloaded, he should focus on message preparation and delegate competing tasks to others.

My unique contribution at Willow Creek is to build our subministries. No one else is so commissioned to help our ministry directors develop their departments. Someone else can type my correspondence, lead singles meetings, or administrate our magazine, but no one else is called to oversee our department leaders.

How do we determine our unique contribution? By considering our gifts, passions, talents, background, personality, and temperament. Given that insight, we can then decide how we can best fulfill the requirements of our particular position.

I try to be a student of myself: Who did God make me to be?

What has he called me to do? The best hours of my day should be given to making that contribution.

After I determine my slice of the circle, I need to look at the remaining tasks and ask, "Who can I find to help me complete the circle?" The key is to find people who feel about their slice the way I feel about mine.

For example, for a number of years I worked with our compensation committee. However, as the staff grew, the salary schedule became increasingly complicated. With no training in this area, I felt terribly inadequate. Yet technically, the responsibility fell in my circle.

At the time, a man in my small group was vice-president of personnel in a major corporation. His Ph.D. and vast corporate experience made salary negotiations a natural for him, and what's more, he enjoyed it.

Today he heads our compensation committee. Because of his expertise, our salary structure is worked out in great detail, and everyone benefits. The staff is better served, the man gets to use his talents to help the church, and I am freed to do the tasks I do best. That happened because I found a leader who feels as strongly about compensation schedules as I do about ministry development.

After determining which tasks to do ourselves and which to delegate, we must decide how much responsibility to give and when to give it. At Willow Creek, we operate on the principle: Faithful with little, faithful with much. We start by giving people a small task or responsibility, and as they prove faithful in that, we give them more.

Sometimes seminary students call and say, "I need an internship. Can I teach at Willow Creek?" We always turn down offers like that. We might offer students the opportunity to lead a small group in their home, and if that works out, expand their leadership role. But we won't bestow great responsibility without a track record of faithfulness and effectiveness in our fellowship. "You start by speaking to five," we tell them, "and then we'll see about fifty."

We expect potential teachers to display strong character, evidence a robust spiritual life, and build relational credibility. Then, if their teaching gift is affirmed, we find a place to use them. The same expectations help us determine what initial administrative or service roles to offer other possible leaders.

While we shouldn't give too much responsibility too soon, it's important to challenge those through whom we work. In fact, it may be more damaging to expect too little of our workers than too much.

Typically people are drawn into leadership because others have noticed their competence in a variety of ways. Usually they're energetic, busy people who have proven they can do a job well. When people like this are bitten by the ministry bug, when they taste the fulfillment of fruitfulness, they want to move ahead.

That's why it's so important to challenge them. To give them too meager a task, to expect too little, to fail to increase their responsibility at the proper time, is a slam. Competent people want to grow into positions of greater responsibility.

Naturally I wouldn't expect someone who has never worked in children's ministry to assume a lead-teacher role in Sunday school. I'd start such a person with a more manageable challenge, perhaps as a small-group leader. However, after a year or so, when the person's competence has been proven, I'd likely make him or her a lead teacher with twenty-five to fifty students.

It's necessary, of course, to talk with workers and monitor their progress. I can't dump a challenge on them and disappear. If I let colleagues drown in their responsibilities, I'm not challenging them; I'm losing them.

Managers need to walk a fine line. They need to move people along at a reasonable rate so they don't feel overwhelmed. But they also need to remember that competent people usually feel most effective when they're stretched, when their responsibilities pull them a step beyond their comfort level. High-potential leaders would rather be roused by challenge than indulged by comfort.

It's that realization that keeps me on my knees. I need divine discernment to know how to challenge workers without overwhelming them.

I tend to be an optimist who sees the best in people and expects the best from them. I want to tell leaders, "You can do it. I know you can." But I can't say that to just anyone. So I don't glean leaders from whatever grows in the field. I prayerfully choose people who display character, spiritual maturity, and competence. Most often, people like that rise to the challenges of ministry.

The Payoff

Recently, circumstances forced me to act as interim director of one of our subministries. Because I already had a full slate of responsibilities, and because the subministry desperately needed a change, I had to find a strategy that would assure a quick turnaround. So I asked myself: *What is going to change this ministry most dramatically in the shortest time?* The answer was clear: key leaders. So I devoted my time and energy to finding potential key leaders.

Focusing on this A priority meant living with other problems, such as inadequate facilities and outdated curriculum. But I couldn't afford to tackle these problems at the cost of my primary task: finding key leaders.

For a while the ministry felt like a huge weight around my neck. Some days I went to my office at 4 A.M. because I couldn't sleep. I was exhausted, I wasn't giving my family what they needed, and the ministry was still in desperate need of change. At best, I was only propping it up.

The final turnaround came when we found the right person to head a major part of the department. The woman we called revolutionized the program. Her volunteers are now enthusiastic, and new people constantly are being attracted to the ministry. The entire program is functioning more smoothly, and details like facilities and curriculum can now be attended to.

Thanks to the contributions of the right leader, a major subministry has undergone a dramatic metamorphosis — and I have become a saner pastor and family man. Now I spend just one afternoon a week on that ministry, coordinating the efforts of the three new primary leaders. I have that luxury because I diligently pursued my A priority of finding leaders through whom I could work. I view that as a major accomplishment of my year.

Had I simply continued as a crutch for the ministry, both the ministry and I would still be limping along. But because I made it a priority to raise up leaders, we now have a healthy department.

When we build ministry that way, everybody wins.

The main thing that keeps volunteers motivated is the sense they are getting more out of their service than they are putting into it.

— Leith Anderson

Motivating and Recruiting Volunteers

Most of the work of the local church is done by volunteers. If the volunteers are ministering effectively, the church is ministering effectively. If they're not, the church is not. It would be difficult, therefore, to conceive of a pastoral responsibility more important than helping volunteers be effective in their ministries.

Working with volunteers in the church involves three basic responsibilities: motivating people, guiding them to the right ministry, and supporting and supervising them as they minister.

Motivating People to Minister

Motivation is not an arcane science. It begins with an understanding of people and what they need. As I have reflected on that, I have developed a few guidelines for motivation within the church.

Use gratitude rather than guilt. Guilt is probably the most powerful motivator in the church. It's quick and effective. When people are desperate to get a job done, they readily employ guilt.

But it also carries a high price tag: resentment. People motivated by guilt develop a subconscious hostility toward the leader and the institution. It is far better to motivate by appealing to gratitude — gratitude to God for all he has done.

I once attended a fund-raising banquet for the seminary from which I graduated. Before I walked in, I had my check made out. For me, at the time, the gift was substantial.

When the banquet host launched his appeal, he told how seven or eight faculty members were paid less than garbage collectors in New York City. (I remember thinking, *So what? Most people in this room are paid less than garbage collectors in New York City.*) His underlying message was, "You, the supporters of the school, don't pay the faculty enough." He was laying guilt on us.

I felt bad. I had wanted to give cheerfully. By the time he'd finished his speech, I had folded my check and put it in my pocket. I was sitting at the head table, but when the ice cream bucket came by, I didn't put in my check.

That host could have motivated by gratitude: "This faculty has had a great impact on your life. You're benefiting from them every day. You've got their books; you've got their lectures; you've got their example. God has blessed you through them. In response to the tremendous gift you've been given, you have an opportunity to say thank you."

If he would have said that, I probably would have torn up my check and written one for more.

The same principle applies to motivating people to volunteer. Some time ago, because of some unusual circumstances that never should have happened, we didn't have an adequate number of Sunday school teachers for the fall program. Some people say that in that situation I should announce, "If somebody isn't going to teach the third graders, we won't have a third-grade class. The pupils can sit in Sunday school with their parents." It's tempting, because it will work; somebody will volunteer. But the volunteer will be somebody who's already overloaded and not gifted to teach third graders. That's an awful approach to the Lord's work.

Even at a time like that, I want to say, "God has taught us wonderful things. He has richly blessed us. Here is a great opportunity God has given us to say thank you, to pass on his blessings to somebody else." That kind of appeal may not have an immediate effect, but for the long term, it's much more effective.

Tap people's existing dissatisfaction. A satisfied need never motivates anyone. If you're totally satisfied, you won't get up in the morning. Before you can be motivated to do anything, you must be dissatisfied. The wonderful thing about the church is that within it there is always an adequate supply of dissatisfaction.

One person is dissatisfied by the loss of identity in a society that treats him more and more like a number. The church can say, "Here is a chance for you to be a significant person in a ministry." Another person is dissatisfied with the church facilities. That becomes a motivation for her to help plan for new facilities.

Our church has an abundance of leaders, and some people are dissatisfied because they want more opportunity to lead. We can say, "Do you want to run things? If you have those skills, great! We'll start another church for which you can provide the leadership." We need to look for ways to harness people's dissatisfaction for ministry.

Give volunteers more than they put in. This could be terribly misunderstood, but the main thing that keeps volunteers motivated is the sense they are getting more out of their service than they are putting into it. If they reach the point where they perceive they are giving more than they're getting, they will quit.

Teachers often say, "I get more out of the class by teaching it than I could by sitting and listening to the lesson." People volunteer so they can experience personal growth, find the satisfaction of serving God, become part of a significant organization, or enjoy camaraderie with other workers. For example, Sunday school teachers hold departmental meetings that they think are designed primarily to plan for the next quarter. But the main purpose of the meeting is to say to teachers, "When you're alone teaching six kids, really you are not alone. You're part of a team. If you become sick or go on vacation, somebody else will take over." The feeling of camaraderie the teachers take from these meetings gives them motivation to continue.

Even if a task involves pain or frustration, when people feel they are gaining significantly from it, they will continue to serve. This means that you can expect a lot from people as long as you "pay" them a lot.

Several years ago our church held a consultation with Lyle Schaller. As part of it, we scheduled a board meeting for one o'clock on Friday afternoon. Although all the board members work on Friday afternoon, everyone was there. Afterward, Schaller commented that having everyone attend wasn't typical. I had never considered the possibility that anybody wouldn't come. I expected the board members to do whatever they had to do — take vacation, if necessary — to be there.

They are willing to do that, however, because their pay is high. Those board members consider board meetings the highlight of their month. In addition, throughout the year, we hold game nights at my house for the elders and their families. If an elder calls, he gets through immediately. I might not change my schedule for somebody else's wedding, but when elders' kids get married, I'm there. I build my life around them and give them preferential treatment, and they know that.

Volunteers' performance remains high when their pay remains high.

Rules for Recruiting

The church has a long history of using people to meet institutional needs. Not only is this approach disrespectful, but it also destroys motivation. Many churches are now learning to reverse the process, to begin not with the institution's needs but with the individual's gifts. Instead of saying, "We need a nursery worker for the fifth Sunday of the month," congregations are learning to ask, "Where should you be serving Jesus Christ?" With this approach, people become better matched to their responsibilities.

Admittedly, this takes time. Wooddale has established a policy that people cannot be asked to serve until their names have been cleared through the staff. This means most of our staff meeting is spent talking about where people can be deployed in ministry. If no one on staff knows a person, a staff member will meet with the person and discuss his or her spiritual development and interests.

Although this approach takes time, it protects people. One volunteer, for example, was urgently needed in our music program. After a pastor visited the home, he reported to staff, "This couple has tensions in their marriage. The commitment to rehearsals wouldn't be good for them right now; they need the time at home." We respected that and determined to find somebody else or shut down that part of the music program.

Frankly, people respond better to an invitation when they discover it comes only after careful consideration by the staff. Suppose, for example, a person is gifted both in music and in working with teens, but because he's starting a new business, he doesn't have time to work in both areas. If we decide the greater need is in youth ministry, the youth pastor would explain to this person that he had been considered for another area but is being asked to take on only one responsibility. Volunteers recognize that as interest in them.

We also offer a Human Resources Program that consists of a seminar, some tests, and an interview with a person skilled in personnel management. The program helps people identify their interests and gifts and look for ways they can use them in the church.

(For some reason, people are willing to admit they have almost any gift except evangelism. To determine who has that gift, we go to an adult Sunday school class, fifty to ninety people who know each other reasonably well. We ask everyone to write down names of people in the group who have the gift of evangelism. Usually, about ten names are repeated. Then a pastor can approach these ten people and say, "The people who have prayed and studied with you, those who know you best, say that you have the gift of evangelism. Would you like to develop that gift and use it more?")

Finally, before a person is approached about a position, a job description is developed that outlines the qualifications, relationships, and responsibilities, including term of service. This again helps people determine if the position is right for them.

Recruiting works better when the invitation comes, not from some full-time church recruiter, but from a person involved in that very ministry. Then the invitation is not, "Will you do this job?" but rather, "Will you join me in doing this job?"

In addition, we work hard to recruit well in advance of the assignment's starting date. Recruiting Sunday school teachers for the fall shouldn't take place in August; it should happen in April. This shows respect for volunteers and gives them time to think and pray about the commitment. The carefully considered commitment is much stronger than the one made hastily.

Normally, a person's first assignment in the church is small. We would never, for example, ask someone to teach an adult congregation if we had not first seen the person teach as a substitute. When we have broken this rule and have guessed incorrectly about a person's ability, we have lost people from the church. Removing people from a position causes them to lose face and to feel they need to find another congregation.

Of course, no matter how thoroughly we do these things, some placements won't work. Sometimes a person will say, "I've tried this for six months, but it's not my gift." When that happens, we need to say, "Fine. Then what should your ministry be?"

Critical Ministries and Critical Roles

When there aren't enough volunteers to staff a program, leaders need to ask, "Is this something we shouldn't be doing?" Theologically, we assume that God will never expect us to do something for which he will not provide the resources. If the resources aren't there, we need to ask, "Should this be dropped?"

The answer lies, in part, in whether the ministry is essential. At Wooddale, for example, morning worship, Sunday school, and child care would be seen as essential. People expect these basic programs in a contemporary American church, so we would not allow these areas to go unstaffed.

But when we didn't have enough men for the men's choir, we dropped the choir. Wooddale organized a ten-kilometer run to increase visibility and outreach in the community, but when we didn't have enough volunteers anymore, we cut the program. These we can live without. Sunday school we cannot.

In addition, some volunteer roles are critical to the life of the church. One is a role I call "the introducer." This person instinctively knows how to connect a visitor with another person, and then he or she moves on to find the next visitor. This person tends to wander through the halls, and we forgive him or her for not coming to worship services. It is important to not tie up the congregation's introducer in teaching Sunday school. Growth depends on having one or more introducers free to do their work.

Other people I look for are the "epaulet men." On the eve of the Battle of Saratoga in 1778, Daniel Morgan led his Morgan's Rifles against the British army led by Gentleman Johnny Burgoyne. Morgan compared his troops and ammunition to the strength of the British, and it was obvious his Rifles were going to lose the battle. So the night before the battle, Morgan gathered his men and said, "Don't waste your shot on those who fight for sixpence a day. Aim for the epaulet men" — the officers, who wore insignia on their shoulders.

The next day, Morgan's Rifles went into battle. When they had a private in their sights, they didn't pull the trigger. They waited until they saw an epaulet man. Following this strategy, Morgan's Rifles won the Battle of Saratoga, and some historians say that was the determining battle of the Revolutionary War.

In the church, we also win or lose by determining who wears the epaulets. If we recognize the leaders and nurture them, all the privates will line up behind them.

The Corporate Ethos

In most churches, the pastor cannot possibly monitor every volunteer position. How, then, can a pastor hope to ensure that people are performing well and conscientiously?

The first and most important thing a pastor does is establish the corporate ethos. Pastors can't manage every person, but they can manage the corporate atmosphere, which in turn will govern those people. Leaders can create an atmosphere that is upbeat, biblically based, rooted in prayer. They can set a climate that includes making proposals before you do things, being accountable, and not operating unilaterally. Those principles come to be understood throughout the organization.

How is this ethos created? By the way the pastor relates to people he or she supervises directly. These people, in turn, treat others the way they have been supervised, and the approach ripples through the organization.

I try to demonstrate to those I supervise that I'm there to serve them. After board meetings, for example, which may go until midnight or one o'clock in the morning, I stay with one or two other people and clean the room. I want to serve that board, so I clean the room so they can get home earlier. And I want to serve the church custodian. One time a custodian said to me, "The board sure leaves the room a mess." I clean the room so he doesn't have a mess the next morning. My hope is that these people will say, "If the pastor will do that for me, I'm going to do that for other people."

Patterns like these eventually duplicate themselves in the organization. For example, our pastors for junior high students and senior high students serve their volunteers so well that they have a waiting list of people to serve.

I never want a volunteer at Wooddale to be recruited and then abandoned. I know that if someone asks a teacher, "Will you teach next year?" but has not talked with that teacher all year long, the teacher will not do it. The only way I can hope to avoid that is to create a corporate ethos that says, "Ongoing support is essential." And I can create that ethos only by continually supporting those people I directly supervise.

I have to remind myself on almost a daily basis that I'm here to help other people succeed. It's in their success that I experience success.

— *Don Cousins*

CHAPTER ELEVEN

Overseeing Staff

One of the most critical responsibilities a church manager has is to build a well-functioning team of workers. In few areas of church life is there more latitude for grand opportunities or dismal failures. A unified team of motivated, well-trained church workers can accomplish just about any ministry objective. But allow that work force to degenerate into factions, or neglect to properly equip workers for their tasks, and a church can wither.

The key to fruitfulness in ministry is fruitfulness in the lives of the individual workers. Therefore, an effective leader must be com-

mitted not only to the organization's goals but also — and especially — to the people making them a reality.

Commitment to Others

Jesus said, "The greatest shall be a servant," and then he
modeled servant-style leadership. What is this kind of leadership?
Simply put, a servant-leader is more committed to the fruitfulness
and fulfillment — the success — of his staff than to his own.

He knows that if his workers bear fruit, if they make a significant impact, they'll be enthusiastic workers. And if they experience
the satisfaction of sensing God's affirmation of their service, they'll
be motivated to encourage others to serve more faithfully, too. So,
the wise leader makes the personal effectiveness of his staff a primary goal, knowing that their fruitfulness and fulfillment will have
a rippling effect.

Ken Blanchard, author of *The One Minute Manager*, describes
such commitment to staff as an upside-down pyramid. Most organizational structures resemble a pyramid, with the CEO at the top,
several levels of middle management as the pyramid broadens, and
then the workers and constituents at the wide base. Blanchard,
however, turns the pyramid on its point, placing the leader on the
bottom. The leader serves the people above him, who in turn serve
those above them, until ultimately the constituents are served. This
way, everyone in the organization benefits.

The rewards of staff-oriented leadership are obvious, but they
don't come without effort. Enhancing the fruitfulness and fulfillment of the people who work for us involves three specific steps:
communicating clear expectations, providing personalized leadership, and offering accurate and honest evaluation.

Communicating Clear Expectations

Peter Drucker has observed that one of the major problems in
business today is that employees often see their primary tasks differently than do their employers. If the worker thinks he's supposed to do one thing and his boss thinks he's to do another,
misunderstanding and conflict are inevitable. Therefore, from the

start, leaders need to make sure expectations are clear. I accomplish that with two tools:

— *A job description.* By that, I mean a general guideline listing what a worker does, not a detailed job outline. A job description that's too broad, such as "oversees the youth ministry," functions more as a position title than a working description. But a grocery list of specific assignments — "plans games at summer camp" or "buys supplies for Sunday school" — makes the job description unwieldy.

A good job description typically lists four to six major responsibilities. For a small-groups director, it might include: recruit new leaders, train them, match them with small groups, and provide them ongoing support. This draws the rough boundaries of the position. It doesn't answer all the questions of specific tasks, but it tells the worker he won't be responsible for securing curriculum or maintaining group directories.

Individual assignments may change. The youth director may plan a retreat over Presidents' Day weekend, but that shouldn't be put into the job description. I'd rather have something like "plans and executes special events to build youth leaders' commitment." The particulars of execution are then left for planning with a supervisor.

— *A monthly listing of priorities.* In my first chapter, I talked about setting A priorities (the top-priority tasks of any particular ministry) and B priorities (ancillary tasks that support the higher priorities). In order to make expectations absolutely clear, every month staff members and I determine together their A and B priorities for the next thirty days.

The amount of input this requires from me depends on the worker's experience and competence. New workers may not know yet what their priorities ought to be, so I help determine them. Experienced staff members simply submit their lists to me to keep me informed. In either case, every month the workers and I both see on paper what their essential tasks are for that month. That keeps us on the same wavelength.

I began spelling out expectations because of how often I found confusion in my workers. I would ask someone well into her job, "Why are you working so hard personally counseling every small-group leader who is struggling?"

"Well," she would reply, "isn't caring for my leaders one of the main things you want me to do — something I really *need* to do?"

I'd have to reply honestly, "No, it's not. I see the priority as designing ways for those leaders to be counseled without having to do it all yourself. Practically speaking, you don't have time for that sort of interaction with the number of leaders you oversee."

I decided it wasn't fair to expect those working for me to read my mind. But if people mutually communicate expectations, they can avoid many problems.

Such communication must, of course, take place in a safe, secure environment. The leader creates this environment through his or her attitude and manner of speaking. I can't say to a staff member, "Here's a list of priorities. I expect you to produce, because I need these tasks finished. I'm going to be checking up on you next month to make sure you're not goofing off." That creates a threatening psychological environment.

Instead, I need to say, "Let's work out your priorities for this month. I'm committed to helping you fulfill these tasks, and I have confidence that you can accomplish great things." That tells staff members I'm on their side and frees them to trust me enough to say willingly, "Hold me accountable."

Occasionally a staff member comes in at the end of the month and says, "I didn't accomplish my goals." If this person is certain I have his or her best interests at heart — that I'm not just waiting to pounce on a mistake — the tenseness of the situation will be greatly mitigated. I can question gently, "Okay. Why not?" without posing a threat.

Such conferences, over a few months, can point out inconsistent work habits, overloaded job descriptions, or inappropriate placement. They help both me and the worker refine or alter the expectations we mutually agree upon. That not only enhances the individual's personal fulfillment and job satisfaction, but it also makes the church's ministry more fruitful. Workers whose time and abilities reflect their priorities usually accomplish their ministry objectives. Over the course of a year — if we're setting the right priorities and the workers are well suited for their positions — they should enjoy significant fruitfulness and fulfillment.

Providing Personalized Leadership

Any parent knows you can't handle every child alike. One disobedient child may need to be rebuked sharply or even spanked. Another crumbles at the mere look of disappointment on his mother's face. Treat both children the same, and one will be crushed or the other unswayed. For parents, the challenge is to know what kind of leadership each child needs.

Likewise, different workers need different kinds of leadership. Some people need a tight leash, others space. Some need to be shown clearly, almost harshly, when they blunder, because their characteristic response to mistakes is a blasé, "Oh well." Others need only a gentle prod, because they've already died a thousand deaths over their error. Giving individuals the type of direction they need is one of the most important aspects of pastoral management.

The best model I've seen for individualized leadership comes from Ken Blanchard's *Leadership and the One Minute Manager.* He calls it *situational leadership.* I prefer to call it *personalized leadership,* because it reminds me that I'm leading people, not just handling situations. Blanchard sees four different leadership styles — direction, coaching, support, and delegation — which should be used according to workers' competence and confidence.

Consider *direction:* If we hire an inexperienced youth pastor straight from seminary, I can hardly delegate the ministry to him; he doesn't yet know how to run a ministry. He lacks confidence because he's never done it before. He comes to our planning meetings with a blank slate and says, "What do I do? Where do I go first?" He may have admirable character, a strong spiritual life, and the basic gifts to get the job done, but he needs point-by-point direction until he gains experience. My job is to give him detailed instructions and basically lead the ministry through him, probably for at least a year.

Coaching is the next step. We can coach workers whose confidence and competence is growing. They come to us with good ideas, and we add some of our own, so that the ministry becomes a joint venture. Coaches are involved enough to know exactly what's happening at each step. The key words for coaches are *affirmation* and *redirection*. Coaches are generous with praise and ready to correct when necessary.

Typically, after a year of coaching, a worker is ready for the third leadership style: *support*. At this point, the worker sets his own agenda; he comes into meetings with his A priorities listed and says, "This is what I'm doing." The supervisor's role is to provide emotional support, encouragement, affirmation, and whatever correction and advice is necessary. The worker being supported knows what to do; he primarily needs to know that someone backs him. In short, for the next year, the leader's role is to be a cheerleader.

The final style is *delegation*, which means the leader turns the ministry over to the individual, for the most part. Reporting continues, but it becomes less frequent; the leash is long.

Delegation doesn't, however, mean abdication. The delegating leader doesn't hand over the responsibility, walk away, and provide no further leadership. He says, "This is your ministry. You build it. But I want to stay in touch. I'm here to serve you."

Obviously, direction, coaching, and support take more of a leader's time than does delegation. That's why it's so tempting to bring people on staff, direct or coach them for a few months, and then say, "All right, go at it." But too often these workers aren't ready for the delegation stage. What's worse is that often delegation slides into abdication; the leader offers no feedback or communication. When that happens, seeds of discord and disarray grow.

Nine years ago, I delegated Willow Creek's high school ministry to Dan Webster. I now meet with Dan for an hour every other week, but I bring a minimal agenda to those sessions. We focus primarily on Dan's agenda. He says, "Here are my ideas (or concerns). Can you give me feedback?" Then we talk about new directions for his ministry, difficulties with his workers, or any other topics he wants to discuss.

In addition to my feedback regarding ministry concerns, Dan

needs my personal involvement in his life. "Ask me how I'm doing at home with my marriage or my kids," he says. "Ask me about my financial decisions, or how I'm handling temptation this week." At this point, Dan's ministry is well under control. He wants me to help him keep his personal life managed as well.

In order to lead properly each person under my management, I have to ask myself, *Based on competence and confidence, does this person need direction, coaching, support or delegation?* I also take that one step further and "contract" with each person about the kind of leadership I will provide, so each knows which to expect. This contract is absolutely vital; it prevents misunderstanding and frustration.

Our people are familiar with Blanchard's system, so usually twice a year I sit down with them and discuss their leadership needs. Newer ministry directors often say, "I need direction."

So I say, "Great! When we meet, I'll do a lot of the talking, and I expect you to ask a lot of the questions."

When a person says, "I'm ready to move on to coaching," I tell him we'll probably split the conversation in meetings. I'll be there to probe and affirm and make sure he doesn't get off the track. In a similar manner, I tell those in the support or delegation stage what to expect.

This contracting process insures that workers get the kind of leadership they need. Supervisors easily offend people by giving them the wrong leadership. If people expect support, and I provide direction, they start to wonder, *Why is he running my ministry and trying to tell me what to do?* On the other hand, if people want direction and all I do is stop by every three weeks and say, "Hey, good job. Keep it up," they're going to feel I'm not leading them.

My goal is for each individual I manage to become independent enough to reach the delegation stage. Usually it takes around three years — one year in each of the preliminary stages — to reach that point. If a person gets stuck and is unable to progress into delegation, it's either because I placed the person wrongly or I haven't supervised sufficiently. My responsibility in that case is to make a careful evaluation and take steps to alter the situation.

A common mistake is to move people through the process too quickly. Generally, staff members tend to slot themselves one step further in the process than they ought to be — a person needing direction, for instance, usually thinks he needs coaching. Too often supervisors, wanting to minimize their output of time, yield to the worker's desire to speed through the process.

But we pay a price when we do this. Almost always a worker prematurely moved into coaching will have to be moved back into direction, and that will foster resentment. A horse that has run free in the pasture inevitably chafes when he's brought back to the stable with a bit in its mouth. Better to keep the horse in the stable until you're sure you want it to run free.

The number of people to whom a supervisor can provide personalized leadership — his span of control — depends on two factors: One, how people are divided among the four stages of supervision, and, two, the supervisor's relational capacity. In other words, I couldn't adequately oversee ten workers who needed direction or coaching, but I could if they moved to support or delegation.

In like manner, I couldn't schedule six to eight conferences a day with leaders under my care; that would drain me emotionally. Being a mild introvert, I have to limit myself to three or four meetings a day if I want to stay emotionally strong.

I learned this lesson the hard way several years ago. Each day I left work exhausted; I had no energy to talk to my wife; I wasn't enjoying my ministry. I finally realized I was overseeing too many people. Although I'm not a total recluse, neither am I a raving extrovert. I can't spread my relational energy that thin without burning out.

Every leader has limited time and relational capacity to invest in personalized leadership. The wise supervisor gauges his span of control by those limits.

Offering Accurate and Honest Evaluation

Good parents openly affirm their children: "We appreciate your good behavior." Or, "You're doing a great job in school."

They also know when to discipline: "If you jump on your bed again, you will be punished." Thus, children know where they stand and what they need to do.

Staff members need similar feedback. They should not be left wondering, *What does my supervisor think of my work? Am I valuable here? Do I make a difference?* The more secure an employee is, the more freedom with which he can operate. That's why leaders need to offer accurate and honest evaluations of those they lead.

I emphasize accurate and honest for good reason. If feedback is inaccurate — all sugar and spice, or clearly out of touch with reality — people lose respect for it. In other words, if I praise efforts for a job poorly done, workers will lose respect for my opinion. Similarly, if feedback is dishonest — if I twist the facts or misrepresent a person's performance — the person naturally will lose trust.

I would rather have my workers know where they stand — even if they stand on the bubble — than have them wondering what I think of their work. They won't have to play guessing games if I care enough to say accurately and honestly where they stand. If people are doing well, they can rejoice in that and work with confidence. If their work is unacceptable, they can determine why and make the necessary changes.

Leaders avoid heartache by providing immediate feedback regarding inferior work. If their initial feedback doesn't bring about the desired change, they need to offer more. Eventually they may have to say, "In spite of my repeated expressions of concern, you are making the same mistakes again and again. If this continues, it may lead to the loss of your job." Yes, that creates insecurity, but ultimately honesty is in everyone's best interest.

Several years ago, we had a talented staff person who turned out excellent work but at the expense of the people with whom he worked. I held conversation after conversation with him expressing appreciation for his work but trying to explain, "Look, you can't go on bruising people as you accomplish your tasks. This has to stop." But nothing seemed to change. The necessary people skills just weren't there.

After much thought and prayer, I found a task-oriented position for him in which he didn't have to work with teams of people. I relieved him of his previous responsibilities and placed him in the new position more suited to his abilities. Nine years later, he continues on our staff as a respected worker, appreciated and loved for his contribution.

In spite of our attempts to be fair, there inevitably will be occasions when the outcome is painful. At those times, fairness may be the most we can expect to offer.

Leading the Team

Workers who are led well and who enjoy fruitfulness and fulfillment can join together to form a strong, smoothly functioning work team. But just like an individual, the team needs to be led. It needs to be encouraged and motivated; it needs to be informed and educated; it needs to have its vision renewed. The avenue through which this happens is the staff meeting.

The staff meeting is similar to the team meeting a coach schedules prior to an important game. Because the coach knows his players are about to confront the opposition, he prepares his agenda carefully. He determines what his team needs most and lists his primary objectives for the meeting.

A church staff faces a challenge far more important than any athletic event, so it's good for pastors to view staff meetings as opportunities to motivate or equip their team for the battle. It's not effective to make a few announcements, work through a brief agenda, and then wonder why workers comes up with so many excuses for missing these weekly meetings.

If staff meetings exist mainly to enable the leader to communicate his agenda, staff morale will suffer. But the leader who thinks, *What does my staff need? How can this meeting help them grow in their effectiveness?* will find the staff eagerly anticipating the meetings. And when staff members feel served by the leader, they will breathe life into the organization.

A leader who recognizes the various functions of staff gatherings will be able to serve his staff's needs better. First is the business meeting, in which the work of the organization is contemplated and communicated. It's the time for making announcements and comparing calendars. Second is the training meeting, where the staff is educated for greater effectiveness. Third is the relational meeting, which builds unity.

Many organizations spend the bulk of their staff time in business meetings. But leaders devoted to building up their workers know that business is their least important staff objective. If they do have to make announcements, they do so in the context of the vision and purpose of the ministry. For instance, I can say, "Well, folks, we need to fill fifteen slots for small-group leaders. Who can we get?" That's an announcement. But I build our common vision if I say, "Friends, our people need to taste what it is to be used of God. One way we can help them do that is to give them a chance to lead small groups . . ."

Recently Bill Hybels, our senior pastor, had to inform the staff of some difficult adjustments in the upcoming year's budget. Bill carefully explained how the adjustments in each department fit into the overall plan, what the implications of not making the adjustments were, and how they ultimately would enhance our efforts. Rather than simply handing out a ledger sheet, he built vision and a spirit of camaraderie as he challenged us to accept the adjustments for the sake of the overall ministry.

Even with such vision-building twists, only about 25 percent of staff-meeting time should be spent on business issues. The bulk of staff time — 50 percent, ideally — should be devoted to training. We have found staff meetings to be the best place for workers to develop skills that lead to increased fruitfulness and fulfillment. We've taken our ministry directors through in-house courses on public speaking, lay counseling, and discipleship.

For instance, we've just worked through a book on leadership. We read it individually. Then in regular staff meetings we broke into small groups to discuss and apply questions I prepared. I try to use variety in the way skills are taught. Some themes work best as talks; some are great for discussion groups. We've had outside experts, such as a professional lecturer on public speaking, lead us through some sessions. Sometimes I ask a staff member who excels in a particular skill to share his insights. Recently the director of our counseling center presented a three-week series on counseling techniques.

Through classes such as these, we've taught our staff how to recruit leaders, build teams, and delegate responsibility. We've even discussed confrontation and conflict resolution.

We try to use 25 percent of our staff time for relationship-building activities. Relational meetings can include anything from a volleyball game to pour-out-your-heart sessions of sharing and prayer. Most of our staff meetings include regular times of sharing and prayer. One department even publishes an in-house newsletter with prayer requests, answers to prayer, and messages of encouragement to other staff members, and the staff prays through it together monthly.

Special events also contribute to the emphasis on the relational. We may have lunch together on the patio or attend a Cubs game. One of our ministry directors actually ran his key lay leaders through a boot-camp-like obstacle course, where they had to work together in order to make it through. Such activities pay large dividends in team spirit.

Devoting time to nurturing staff members' competence and interpersonal relationships says we value them, not just their ministry output. Organizing staff meetings to meet their needs is one of the most important ways we can serve our workers.

Results

Overseeing a staff is hard work. It takes time and energy to communicate clear expectations, provide personalized leadership, and offer accurate and honest evaluation. It takes even more time and energy to forge individual workers into a smoothly functioning work team.

Leadership is particularly draining when it involves making tough decisions. But the rewards validate the efforts. Some time ago I received a letter from a staff member that reads in part (with names changed):

I wanted to encourage you regarding something you

said in ministry directors' meeting yesterday. As you put it, "It is better to do the painful task of redirecting someone now than to let it go on, making the task more painful in the future and the rebuilding process that much longer."

One reason that's true is that those under such misplaced people also suffer. For the two years I worked under Ted, I was in agony. Though he tried to do the right things, his methods left me hurting (to this day). Part of what devastated me was the thought that you must not have thought much of me to have left me in the care of such an inept person. . . .

Your moving Ted out and putting Jeff in restored my faith in you. Now I know you care, because you provided me with a leader who can do the job well.

I don't know how much longer I could have worked under the old conditions. But I'm still here, more fulfilled than ever — and dare I say more fruitful? — and it's because you faced up to a tough management decision and did the right thing even though it caused you pain.

Thanks for enduring that for me.

A letter like that reminds me that the decisions I make have repercussions that go far beyond the people I oversee directly. It's the rippling effect again. My effectiveness in leading them determines their effectiveness in leading others, and eventually that impacts the entire congregation.

That's why the way I lead is so important. The people under my supervision need to be built up and encouraged, so they can enjoy maximum fruitfulness and fulfillment, and produce that in others. If I don't provide leadership to bring that about, I'm not doing what I've been called to do.

Even the wisest of churches ends up with ineffective employees, who need supervision, redirection, and perhaps termination. Mastering church management means, then, learning to hire and, yes, fire.

— Arthur DeKruyter

CHAPTER TWELVE
Hiring and Firing

A pastor manages people — some volunteers and some employees. Even the small church usually finds room in its budget to hire a part-time secretary or janitor. These are staff the pastor must oversee. And it doesn't take long to learn that staff members — even part-time — if ineffectively managed, can undercut a church's ministry. Effectively managed, they can strengthen a church's ministry immeasurably.

Effective management of staff begins with the hiring process. A church will not be tripped up as much if this first step is taken well. But even the wisest of churches ends up with ineffective employees, who need supervision, redirection, and perhaps termination. Mastering church management means learning to hire and, yes, fire.

Before Hiring: Some Questions

Before we get to specifics, however, a few preliminary questions must be answered.

● *When is it time to replace volunteers with employees?* Some believe that the ideal church should manage itself with only volunteers. That would develop lay leadership and be good for the budget besides! Ideal or not, most churches quickly see that lay leadership needs to be supplemented with hired staff. But how do you know *when* to supplement? When is it time to hire someone to do what has been a volunteer position? We hire when I see one of three situations develop.

First, we hire if the volunteer becomes overworked in his or her job. Early in one of my churches, I discovered that the treasurer of the church, a man at ease with numbers and spreadsheets, had to spend twenty hours a week doing the church's books. That was unfair to him and unfair to his family. So we brought on a part-time bookkeeper.

Second, we hire when we cannot find in our volunteer pool the skills we need for a job. When skills are inadequate, quality and excellence are sacrificed. That means that people will suffer spiritually in the long run. To be fair to our congregation we hire people with expertise if we cannot find an "expert" volunteer.

We have a retired businessman who has been chairman of our missions committee for six years now. Because he's retired he is able to put in twenty or more hours a week without burdening himself. He even pays his own way to travel around the mission field. His ministry of missions has grown so much during his tenure that when he "retires" from the missions committee, we will probably hire someone to take his place. His ministry and skills have become so important to the church that we simply will not want that ministry to flounder.

Sometimes we move back and forth between volunteers and employees. For example, teaching adolescents requires specific skills. Sometimes a member of the church will have those skills. If so, that member can teach the high school class. But if no member can do that, we hire a teacher, perhaps a member of a parachurch organization. And if later we gain a member who can teach youth, we go back to a volunteer system.

The point is, if the job requires expertise, we find the "expert" in the church. If we can't, we consider hiring from outside.

Third, we hire when our volunteer system breaks down. The church, like other volunteer organizations, constantly struggles with this one. We recently had three volunteers who agreed to chaperone a young people's trip call three days before the trip and say: "Sorry, we can't go. Something's come up." You cannot run a church that way. When our church decides that we need consistent quality in a program, we hire. Because the hired staff person has covenanted with us to be productive, we can demand a greater level of accountability. We cannot do that with volunteers.

● *When should we move from lay to ordained staff?* This question focuses on the difference between lay and clergy staff. When can a lay person handle a position, and when is it necessary to have a clergy person?

Naturally, this discussion hinges on one's view of ordination. I believe ordination signals that a person has been called by the Lord through the church to minister to and through the church. Theologically, that may be enough, but administratively we need more criteria. We need to consider the function of the position. Some positions require that the person function as an ordained person, one who can marry and bury, who represents the church, or who can work in an ecumenical capacity. Not all of these functions absolutely require ordination, but given the expectations of people, it may be best to hire a clergy person.

In many situations, of course, ordination doesn't matter. Take our young-adult ministry, for instance. Twice we've put a young lay person in charge of our college and young-singles ministries. In both cases, as time went on, each of the young men desired more training and began attending seminary while he worked here. After seminary both received ordination and stayed on staff as clergy.

• *Do we hire within or outside the membership?* Our first general principle is this: You don't pay members of your own family. We expect members of the church to offer themselves freely to serve. And when our board decides, for the reasons stated above, that it's time to hire, we hire outside the membership.

That principle cannot, of course, be applied across the board. Choir directors and associate ministers, for example, are paid and they are members of the church. But their jobs require them to be intensely involved in the life of the church. Jobs with limited congregational involvement (functional jobs: janitor, secretary) are jobs that should be given to people outside the congregation. If the talent were available, we would rightly expect members to contribute their time in those jobs. Of course, at times the line between these two categories gets fuzzy.

Our second principle: we never hire someone we can't fire. That's a crude way of saying that we want to be able to exercise free judgment about an employee's work and perform our administrative responsibility to the congregation. This rule encourages us to look first outside the church when we need to hire.

Our third principle: Don't hire within the congregation if it's going to hamper effective ministry. This applies particularly to the position of church secretary. Church members, especially those coming to a pastor for counseling, are less inhibited about doing so if they don't know the secretary socially. They don't want to walk out of my office in tears when a member whom they'll see in worship or at a picnic on Saturday sits at the front desk. Naturally, this is a tension when you're first starting a church and must use volunteers as secretaries. Then you have to live with the tension.

• *Who should do the hiring?* In our church polity, the formal hiring is done by the board of trustees or delegated to a person or group. But as important as this structure is, it is vital to allow the staff member who will supervise the new position to define the position and do the initial screening. He reports, in turn, to his supervisor, usually me. But since he will have the primary relationship with the person hired, it's important he have the first say about who gets hired.

So, if the Christian education pastor needs an associate in children's ministries, he personally will select that person before bringing him or her to me. He has the opportunity to find someone compatible. Furthermore, as the education expert, he has more competence to judge the person's abilities. I do, however, keep in touch through the entire process; I look at the job description, suggest changes, and offer cautions here and there. Then, when he comes to me with a candidate, I interview the person, as does the board upon my recommendation. For people such as interns and assistants to pastors, those serving between the staff and congregation, the board interview is more of a review. The critical interview has already been done by the staff member and me. But I have found that even these candidates need to meet the board to get an idea of what the board expects of them. It's a good introduction and reminder of accountability.

● *Whom do you hire first?* My guiding principle is that an organization ought to invest in that part of the organization that will immediately affect the community it seeks to reach.

In our approach, we bring people together primarily through worship. Consequently, the first person we hired was a part-time organist and choir director. I was convinced that if the worship service on Sunday were to be done with excellence, our church could make it in this community. Worship was our showpiece, the community's introduction to Christ Church of Oak Brook. So as soon as we were able, we hired someone who could help us worship with excellence.

Some believe a church should hire a secretary first to free up the pastor's time. In my experience, however, there are always people in the congregation who will give a few hours for secretarial work and do a fine job. But finding someone to lead music with excellence is something else. If I have the money, I'd rather spend it to hire those who will impact the community.

● *What benefits should we offer full-time, nonordained staff?* Since most ministers are offered a variety of benefits, and since many denominations require them, I will focus my thoughts on the part of the staff that may get overlooked.

We believe it is an absolute requisite these days to offer all full-time staff adequate health care. The church cannot expect devotion from its staff if it is not willing to care for them when they fall ill. The first benefit we offer, then, is health care for the staff members and their families. We consider it a moral obligation.

We once sponsored an overseas missionary who contracted Hodgkin's Disease. We found out that the parachurch organization for which he worked had no health care for him or his family. Fortunately, a doctor from our congregation took him into his home, and we took care of him. But we also suggested to the parachurch organization that their policies were irresponsible.

Second, we insist that our heads of households participate in a retirement program. We don't want our people to reach retirement age and suddenly realize they haven't laid anything away. If they don't know anything about it, we'll offer them counsel and set up a program for them. If the staff person pleads, "I need my money this year; don't put it in a pension fund," we politely refuse.

Those are the minimum benefits we think every full-time employee of the church should have. We will not support even missionaries unless the organization for which they work has that same commitment.

● *What are the legal ramifications of hiring — and firing?* A lot of legal issues arise today that we never used to have to think about. Our board recently was discussing, for example, whether it would be possible to have a mandatory retirement age of 65 years. We found out, however, that such a policy would be illegal. If we want to do that, the church has to get an agreement from the person at the time of hiring. On top of that, there are matters like liability and severance pay — so many matters that I could not begin to discuss them here.

Suffice it to say, we have an attorney on our board who helps us in this respect. I believe it would be wise for even a small church to have access to an attorney whom it could consult from time to time. In today's world it's a must.

Hiring: What to Look For

When hiring, whether for a ministry or support position, we

look for three things: Christian commitment, compatibility, and a combination of competence-dedication-vision.

● *Christian commitment*. Deep Christian commitment is a given, of course, with full-time ministry staff. But how much Christian commitment should we expect of people in support positions — secretaries and janitors?

I think it's highly important, for theological but also practical reasons. Christian commitment makes people better workers. They're more likely to see their job as a vocation, a calling. The church usually cannot offer salary and benefits that secular institutions can — especially for people of talent, the type of people we want. So skilled people who are looking for work in the church are likely to have a significant level of Christian commitment to begin with. After all, they are willing to sacrifice financially in order to work in a place that seeks to serve and glorify Christ.

● *Compatibility*. Another characteristic I look for during the hiring process is compatibility, both doctrinal and personal. Of course, the more ministry oriented the position, the more compatibility we expect.

Doctrinal compatibility is especially important with ministerial staff. But personal compatibility is just as important for us. We could not have, for example, an independent, strong-headed person working in the education department here who expressed publicly his disagreements with the music program. We're looking for team players, people who can do their job with excellence, trust others to do theirs, and work with them cooperatively.

Naturally, it is difficult to discern compatibility in the all-too-brief interview process. But there are signals that tip us off regarding the person's ability to get along with other people.

For example, we look at the candidate's length of stay in other positions. If a person moves every three or four years, I want to know why. It takes one to two years to find out someone isn't doing well and another year or two to help him relocate. So a three- or four-year stint at a job may not indicate a good working relationship.

If this is someone I'm hiring, I'll ask my staff to meet with the person. I urge the candidate to probe each of my other staff members about me, this organization, and our style of management. I think it's important for the candidate to talk confidentially with the people with whom he or she will be working. And I'll want the staff's impressions of the person's compatibility.

In addition, appearance can tell me a great deal. The candidate must be able to read the culture to which he or she will be ministering. If we discover that we've got a child of the sixties, who doesn't like organizations and institutions, Oak Brook is no place for that person. Our congregation consists of institutional people. We want our staff to love these people, not condemn them. So we feel the candidate must fit the church's culture, and that includes the way he or she dresses.

In addition, particularly when it comes to ministerial staff, we also look for compatibility of competence. We don't like to have a Ph.D. in one department and a Bible school graduate in another. We strive for a match in quality and maturity across the board.

In short, compatibility means more than just being able to get along.

● *Competence-dedication-vision.* After compatibility, we aim to hire people who combine these three qualities. We once interviewed a man who had a good track record. Everything went fine through the interview process, so we brought him on. For the first few months he worked hard and did well.

In six months, however, we began to notice a trend. He seemed to have decided that this was a nice place to retire at an early age. He would arrive at nine o'clock in the morning with his newspaper, shut his door, and read it. He began his appointments about ten o'clock and made a few calls. But every afternoon at four-thirty, he walked out his door. And if he possibly could avoid coming back at night, he'd avoid it. He would tell people, "I'm sorry, but I don't work after four-thirty." If he had to attend a meeting at night, he would leave the office at noon.

He wasn't putting in the time and energy the job demanded. The rest of the staff started to come to me and say, "Hey, this fellow isn't pulling his load." You can't hook up a team of horses and have one of them dragging behind.

We want our ministerial staff to be leaders who develop a vision for their departments. Then we can turn them loose.

I've noticed that compatibility and competence make an outstanding combination. Not only are staff members doing great things in their departments, but when we get together, that energy and creativity tends to sharpen each of us. In addition, that combination seems to encourage longevity on my staff. Nobody wants to leave a place where team play and individual excellence are encouraged.

We also look for a high level of competence with our support staff. Of course, when I hire a secretary, I look for more than mere secretarial skills. I learn a great deal about my staff and congregation through my secretary. The church office is a hub of church life. An alert secretary can pick up a lot. So I often will ask her opinion about things that effect the congregation. My secretary needs to type, but she also needs wisdom.

How to Get an Honest Reference

In looking for Christian commitment, compatibility, and competence, the church often has to rely on evaluations of those who have worked with the candidate. But evaluations can be notoriously deceptive. First, the candidate is going to list only references who will evaluate him positively. In addition, most who write evaluations hesitate to speak negatively about the person they evaluate. Yet, in spite of these handicaps, I think it's possible to get an honest evaluation. It's not only possible; it's vital.

To begin with, we don't just read the references' letters; we interview them. I can catch things on the telephone — hesitancy or enthusiasm. I also try to find a friend or acquaintance who knows somebody where this person has been. Often I find such people, especially if I dig a little. This person can give me insights the references won't give. Trying to locate someone for whom the candidate worked two or three situations ago also helps. Their superiors tend to be far more honest with the passing of time.

All this may seem like a lot of trouble. But it saves our church much grief down the road if I will take the time at the beginning.

When the Job Isn't Getting Done

From time to time I suspect a staff member may be malfunctioning. This hardly constitutes evidence for firing, although it may eventually lead to it. What are the steps to take before that drastic measure is called for?

● *Quietly investigate.* As soon as I suspect trouble, I begin keeping my ear to the ground. I ask questions of secretaries or other staff. But I do so quietly, subtly, in a casual manner: What's going on with So-and-so? How are his groups doing? Anything new coming on line? What's happening in the department? How many people were in his last class?

● *Meet with staff.* If two or three staff members suggest there are problems with the person in question, I call a meeting of the entire staff, not including the person in question. I'll ask how serious the problem is. Is it worth looking into, or should I just forget about it? If something should come out, that's when it does.

● *Encourage staff to be honest with the person.* Next I encourage the rest of the staff to tell the person, in a tactful way, the problems he's causing them — when he didn't come to a meeting, or when he stood somebody up, or when he avoided a job that they got stuck with. They shouldn't sit around trying to be nice. In the long run, it's better to talk with the person. And often honesty from peers will solve the problem.

● *Probation.* If that doesn't work, I will have an interview with the person, and I will ask for his or her perspective regarding the problem.

Unless something unexpected comes to light, I will explain to the person that without a change in the next six months, he will be dismissed. I list the specific things that trouble me and the ways those things can be cleared up. I explain that we will have regular meetings to evaluate his work along the way.

One former staff member didn't realize that we expected creative leadership from him. He thought he was to follow the pattern of a predecessor and merely maintain the status quo. When his creativity and aggressiveness began to lag, I called him in and said, "I think things could be going better." He listened intently. He wanted to know what he should do differently.

When I told him, he said, "You give me three or four months, and I'll turn this thing around." I asked for some goals and objectives, which he had for me within a week. I said, "Okay. You meet those goals, and you're back in business."

He came back in four months and had met every one of them. He hadn't realized it was his prerogative to be aggressive. All he needed was honest feedback.

● *Bring in the board.* By this time, I have informed the trustee board of what I'm doing. If they have any questions, they talk to the person. And before I decide on a course of action, I will ask the board for advice. Those men, gifted in management and administration, often counsel me wisely on how to handle malfunctioning people.

On one occasion I asked a staff member, who used his time poorly, to keep a log of his next thirty days. I wanted to know when he came to work, how many hours he put in, whether he studied at home, where he went. I wanted to know everything he did from the time he got out of bed until the time he went back to bed. My board encouraged me to do that. It turned out to be an excellent approach.

Naturally, they are pledged to confidentiality. Nothing of this sort gets out of the board, not even to their families.

● *Get the person to tell you what you said.* When I talk with someone about job performance or about an unpleasant decision, I ask the person to repeat what I said. Because they are caught emotionally off balance in this situation, people may hear things differently than I say them.

Once, because of her poor performance with a particular age level, I had to ask a church school teacher to teach a different class. She left the office and immediately called a friend and said, "Can you imagine! After fourteen years of teaching Sunday school, I got fired." Word got back to me, "Why did you fire So-and-so?" I hadn't fired her, I'd merely told her she was being moved to a different class. Letting people summarize what I've said during the interview eliminates needless misunderstandings.

Dismissing a Staff Member

What happens at the end of six months when things have not improved? What are the next steps?

● *Give time to find new work.* First, we tell the person he will no longer work here after a certain date, but we let him stay on staff three to nine months at full salary and with freedom to interview. During that time, he maintains his responsibilities in the church.

The only people who know he's been terminated are those who have agreed that he ought to be fired: the board and staff. If he makes trouble in the congregation or lets it out that he's being terminated, he is asked immediately to clean out his desk. In that case, he is given only an abbreviated period of full pay.

On those occasions when our congregation has learned of a firing, it hasn't caused a problem. The congregation has enough confidence in the board to know that if someone has been fired, it was probably best. The few people who have questions will ask a staff member what's going on. When we explain the steps we took and the offers we made, they end up agreeing with our decision. Because we have a defensible process, we're not as vulnerable.

● *Give a gracious farewell.* When the person finds another position, we announce to the congregation that he has received a call to another place. We publicly wish him well, although we won't necessarily praise him for all he did here.

● *Give fair references.* As this staff person interviews elsewhere, his potential employers may phone me for a reference. What am I supposed to say?

I put the ball in their court. I ask, "What exactly do you want to know about this person?" I make them ask specific questions. I do not volunteer any information. And then I answer honestly.

For example, if the employer asks if the staff member is a competent youth minister, I ask, "What are you expecting of your youth minister?" If he says, "Well, I'm expecting him to visit with kids and lead singing during the meetings," I might respond, "I think he could lead singing successfully, but he tried visiting kids and it didn't work. I can't tell you if he could do that for you successfully or not, but it wasn't very successful here."

So I try to be honest and yet give the staff member all the opportunity I can. Sometimes other organizations aren't looking for the same things we are, and a person who failed here can succeed elsewhere.

Even Good Administrators Sometimes Lose

In spite of thoughtful procedure and compassionate manage-ment, things sometimes go wrong. Even if I do everything right, I sometimes lose, or the church may suffer a setback. I may wind up with an angry member who leaves the church over a personnel decision I've made. We may end up hiring a staff member who turns out to be incompetent. Sometimes the problem is the hardheaded-ness of a board member or my inability to predict the future, not a lack of administrative competence.

So in the midst of these tough personnel decisions, I try to do what is best for all concerned, not simply what will make me look successful. My job is not to guarantee success or boast a flawlessly run organization. My job is to make the best decisions I can, and trust that God, in the long run, will use them to build his kingdom.

In the final analysis, church management comes down to service: the willingness to do what it takes to make ministry happen through others.

— *James D. Berkley*

Epilogue

When all is said and done, more is said than done." We've all heard the quip, and often it's true.

But it's not true about the three pastors imparting the many words of this book. True, they've said much, but they've done even more. They have developed or refined the strategies they have disclosed in this book — and they've made them work. The scope and effectiveness of each man's ministry speak volumes about the ways he is practicing church management.

Their effectiveness might even be intimidating. So it's somehow comforting to be reminded that not everything runs smoothly, even for those who have developed their church-management skills to high levels.

You'd be shocked to know, for example, that Willow Creek's FAX machine *ran out of paper* right in the middle of an important, last-minute transmission from our office. Yes, despite Don Cousins's administration, it ran out of paper.

At Wooddale Church, under Leith Anderson's management, a recent churchwide picnic was carefully planned and well advertised. Yet a few days before, only a handful of people had bought tickets for it.

And Arthur DeKruyter, a master of efficiency, nonetheless returned two revised chapters almost twenty-four hours late. (But we forgave him because he improved our editing by catching some prepositions, which one is not supposed to end sentences with.)

My point is that these gifted leaders are like you and me and other Christian leaders throughout the centuries who have given their lives to the leadership of God's people. Not everything goes smoothly in the process of leading and managing. But they have continued to think and dream. They've ventured. They've committed themselves. They've achieved. They've dusted themselves off after mistakes. They've persevered.

Why? To serve God through serving his people, and to serve his people by making them effective in ministry. In the final analysis, church management comes down to service: the willingness to do what it takes to make ministry happen through others. And the final reward is not a bigger office with a leather-covered chair. No, it's much better. It's the Lord's "Well done, good and faithful *servant.*"